Henry Summer Maine

International Law

A Series of Lectures delivered before the University of Cambridge, 1887

Henry Summer Maine

International Law
A Series of Lectures delivered before the University of Cambridge, 1887

ISBN/EAN: 9783337233068

Printed in Europe, USA, Canada, Australia, Japan

Cover: Foto ©Suzi / pixelio.de

More available books at **www.hansebooks.com**

THE WHEWELL LECTURES

INTERNATIONAL LAW

A SERIES OF

LECTURES DELIVERED BEFORE THE
UNIVERSITY OF CAMBRIDGE
1887

By HENRY SUMNER MAINE, K.C.S.I.

LATE MASTER OF TRINITY HALL, CAMBRIDGE, AND
MEMBER OF THE INDIAN COUNCIL

LONDON
JOHN MURRAY, ALBEMARLE STREET
1888

PRINTED BY
SPOTTISWOODE AND CO., NEW-STREET SQUARE
LONDON

NOTICE.

THE following Lectures were delivered before the University of Cambridge, in Michaelmas Term 1887, by the late Sir Henry S. Maine, then Professor of International Law on the foundation of Dr. Whewell. They are printed from the manuscript, partly written in his own hand, and throughout corrected by him for delivery, but not prepared for publication. The sheets have been passed through the press by Mr. Frederic Harrison and Mr. Frederick Pollock, both of Lincoln's Inn, who were appointed two of Sir H. Maine's executors. They have not thought it their duty in any way to alter the draft of the Lectures, except so far as was needed to clear the sense of an occasional passage, which in the copy as it stood was obscure or plainly defective. Titles to the Lectures and an Index have also been added.

LINCOLN'S INN: September, 1888.

CONTENTS.

INTERNATIONAL LAW.

LECTURE I.

ITS ORIGIN AND SOURCES.

THE eminent man who founded the Whewell Professorship of International Law laid an earnest and express injunction on the occupant of this chair that he should make it his aim, in all parts of his treatment of the subject, to lay down such rules and suggest such measures as might tend to diminish the evils of war and finally to extinguish war among nations.

These words of Dr. Whewell, which occur in his will and in the statute regulating his professorship, undoubtedly contain both a condemnation and a direction. International Law in its earlier stages was developed by a method of treatment which has been applied to many important subjects of thought when their growth has reached the point at which they are included in books—to theology, to morals, and even, in some cases, to positive private law. Writers of

B

authority who have gained the ear of the learned and professional classes follow one another in a string, each commenting on his predecessor, and correcting, adding to, or devising new applications for, the propositions he has laid down. For a considerable time International Law, as the words are commonly understood, had to be exclusively collected from the dicta of these authoritative writers, who, however, differed from one another materially in their qualities and defects. At the head and at the foot of the list two names are often conventionally placed, first that of Grotius, who was born in 1583, and died in 1645, and last that of Vattel, who was born in 1714 and died in 1767. Of both these writers it may be confidently asserted that the rules and propositions which they laid down did tend to diminish the evils of war and may possibly help to extinguish some day war among nations. But of the residue of this class of publicists, it must be confessed that some were superficial, some learned and pedantic, some were wanting in clearness of thought and expression, some were little sensitive to the modifications of moral judgment produced by growing humanity, and some were simply reactionary. As these lectures proceed I may be able to point out to which class, and for what reasons, the writer immediately before us belongs.

Meantime I may be allowed to pause and say that at first sight it seems hopeless to discharge in our

day the responsibility which Dr. Whewell has laid
on his professor. What teacher of Law, public or
private, considering what we see around us, can hope
to suggest the means of controlling, and still less
of weakening and destroying, the prodigious forces
which seem now to make for war? The facts and
the figures alike appear to point to an enormous
growth of these forces in volume and strength. The
middle year of this century was the thirty-fifth of the
long peace which began in 1815—a peace which was
not quite unbroken, for there were some intervals of
petty local war, but which was as long as any which
existed since Modern Europe began, and a peace which
was fruitful in every sort of remarkable result.

That generation may be said to have had a dream of
peace. It looked forward to a time when, in the words
of the great poet who was then beginning to exercise influence over it, ' The war drum should beat no longer
and the battle flag should be furled.' And in 1851 an
event occurred which has since then been somewhat
vulgarised by repetition, the establishment of the
first of the Exhibitions of Art and Industry. It
seriously added to the belief that wars had ceased ;
strife in arms was to be superseded by competition
in the peaceful arts, controversy was to be conducted
by literary agencies and no longer by arms. As a
poet and prose-writer then still living put it, ' Captain
Pen had vanquished Captain Sword.'

But the buildings of this Temple of Peace had hardly been removed when war broke out again, more terrible than ever. First came the Crimean War in which this country was a principal belligerent ; then followed the frightful struggle of the Indian Mutiny in which England was solely concerned. Shortly afterwards the Government of the new French Empire attacked the Governments established in Italy by the Treaty of Vienna, and soon the whole of the Italian arrangements set up by that Treaty were destroyed. Before long, the United States of America, supposed to be preserved from war by a sort of homely common sense, were torn asunder by the war of secession, which, proportionately to its continuance, was the costliest and bloodiest of wars. In no long time the German arrangements which were established at Vienna fell in pieces through a quarrel between the chief German powers. Almost the other day there came the French and German war and the struggle between the Russians and the Turks—contests which unveiled the bases of quarrels of which we have not seen the end : namely, the historical rivalry between the French and Germans, and the most hopeless of all the problems which the civilised world has to solve, the contest provoked by the inevitable break-up of the Turkish Empire.

The immediate causes of these wars can of course be traced ; but to believers in the permanent return of peace they were a bitter deception. Even more alarming than the return of war was the intrusion of war into peace. After the defeat of Jena, the limitation of their army which the Emperor Napoleon forced upon the Prussians produced a system of which the effect was to teach the Western world a new method of military organisation. The whole population of a country was passed through the ranks of armies. As in the most ancient days, the young men primarily fought, after them came the next above them in age, after these their elders ; all of them knew, and now know, the use of arms, and nobody escapes the necessity for fighting in particular contingencies, except either the very old or the very young. The figures are exceedingly astonishing. When Russia was rising to the height of military reputation which she gained in 1812 and 1813, she had always a difficulty in bringing as many as 100,000 men into the field ; now she is said to contain six millions of armed men. The most energetic effort which was ever made by France to arm her population was in 1813, after the retreat from Moscow and before Napoleon's surprising campaigns within the limits of France herself were commenced. The number of men which Napoleon with all his lieutenants led to combat from France, Italy, and the Confederation of the Rhine (to which were added the disengaged garrisons of French soldiers) was almost exactly equal to the number of men which France at this moment regards as that of her army when on a strictly peace footing.

'War,' says Grotius, in a remarkable passage in which he shows his dissent from the opinions of the preceding age, 'war is not an art.' Nowadays not only is it an art requiring a long apprenticeship and equipped with a multitude of precise rules, but besides this it is the mother of new arts. The whole science and art of explosives, which has occupied the inventive genius of civilised lands for about twenty years, is of warlike origin ; and an apparently most peaceful art, hydraulic engineering, is said to owe its remarkable modern development to the study of the means of lifting and working great naval guns. Guns of long range were first tried in the field during the Crimean war, when they were on the whole pronounced to be a costly failure. But we have some very remarkable evidence at this moment of what they have come to, supplied partly by a Committee of the House of Commons appointed to consider the army estimates, and partly by the report of a Royal Commission appointed to investigate the subject of naval patterns, or in other words, the mode in which new inventions are dealt with by the civil and military officers of our government. The Director-General of Artillery stated to the Parliamentary Committee that the increase in army

estimates which was due to the advance of military
science, began in 1882–83, when breech-loading guns
were finally adopted.   The cost of the steel gun
was a third more than that of the old wrought-
iron tube, but this cost increased till in the case
of the 100-ton gun it exceeded 19,000*l*., while the
cost of the projectile, which once was rather over
7*l*., now reaches at least 150*l*.   All the treasure and
all the labour and all the skill expended nowadays
on ships and fortifications appear to end in this.
Each of the most modern guns is likely to cost
20,000*l*.   It fires a charge of powder and shot weigh-
ing about a ton and a quarter.   Each charge costs
150*l*.   It thus happens that one of the large guns
used in the ships in which the great naval victories
of England were won at the end of the last century
and the beginning of the present did not cost much
more than a few charges of powder and shot fired off
in a gun of the present day.   Nor is this all the
story.   After a gun of the present day has fired 150
shots it is so damaged by the labour and strain it
has undergone that it must be repaired.   This short
effective existence is the result of the extreme
delicacy with which it has been endowed by modern
art.   I repeat, then, my question—when the forces at
work are so enormous, how shall they be controlled,
diminished, or reduced by a mere literary agency ?

Some consolation may be found in a position

which it is all the more necessary to insist upon
because it is not quite in harmony with the assumptions made by some famous writers, presently to be
discussed, who are more associated than any others
with the origin of International Law. Most of them
thought that mankind had started from a condition
of innocent peace. It was man's depravity which
had interrupted this state and had produced virtually
universal and unceasing war. There can be no question that this proposition reverses the truth. It is
not peace which was natural and primitive and old,
but rather war. War appears to be as old as mankind, but peace is a modern invention. Our intelli-
gence is only just beginning to enable us to penetrate
the clouds which rest on the farther verge of history,
but what does seem clear to trained observation is
the universal belligerency of primitive mankind. Not
only is war to be seen everywhere, but it is war more
atrocious than we, with our ideas, can easily conceive.

Take one example, the practices concerned with
the treatment of the wounded and of prisoners. At
first there are signs which cannot be mistaken
that the prisoner and the wounded man are not
only killed but tortured before being put to death.
The still savage races from whom most has been
learned as to the original usages and conditions
of men are the North American Indians and the
aborigines of Australia. That the North American

Indians tortured their prisoners before putting them
to death is one of a number of facts very familiar
to us which have made their way into literature.
One branch of this race, the Mexicans, attained to a
certain degree of civilisation, but it is also matter
of familiar knowledge that the Mexicans put their
prisoners to death with the greatest cruelty almost
in hecatombs, and that the practice with them had
acquired a religious sanction.   As to the Australians,
it has been observed that they have inherited the
animal instinct which leads them even to torture
their game after it is captured and before it is killed.
The English school-boy has often been shocked by
the concluding passage in a Roman triumph when
the gallant enemy, who had been led in the pro-
cession, was not only killed but flogged.   When we
come to mediæval war these cruelties have disappeared, and, though the suffering of the wounded and
of prisoners was great, it seems to have been due
rather to ignorance and carelessness than to cruelty.
It is said that at the battle of Agincourt only one
man who had any knowledge of medicine or surgery
was present, the functionary who was the predecessor
of the official now known as the King's Staff Surgeon.
   The only influences which at the beginning of
history seem to put an end to war on a large scale
are influences which have been much maligned
and to which some injustice has been done.   The

conventionally revised history of the world begins
with the formation of certain great empires, the
Egyptian, the Assyrian, the Median, and the Persian.
No doubt they were a result rather of man's rapacity
than of his humanity. The object of their founders
was to gratify ambitious display on a great scale and
to increase the area from which they could take their
taxes ; but nevertheless no one could say how much
war they extinguished by the prohibition, which they
undoubtedly carried out, of hostilities among the
various sub-divisions of their subjects. The latest of
these Empires which conferred similar benefits on
mankind in the West was the Roman Empire.
During the long Roman peace not only did bloodshed practically cease, but the equality of the sexes,
the mitigation of slavery, and the organisation of
Christianity made their appearance in the world.

When, however, one of these empires breaks up,
the old suffering revives. ' Give peace in our time, O
Lord,' is a versicle in the Anglican Liturgy which
is said to date from the rupture of the Empire, that
is from the time when the Empire was breaking up
into kingdoms occupied by barbarian races. It is
obviously a prayer for an unusual and unhoped-for
blessing. In the East the amount of bloodshed
prevented by the Chinese Empire is incalculable.
Independently of any other benefits, which the
Indian Empire may confer on the collection of

countries which it includes, there is no question that were it to be dissolved, or to fall into the hands of masters unable to govern it, the territories which make it up would be deluged with blood from end to end. As the history of modern Europe proceeds there are moments when old controversies seem to have been exhausted and fighting is to a certain extent relaxed, but then some great difference arises between men—the wars of religion, for example, commence—and Europe is again full of bloodshed.

There are other facts at first sight of smaller apparent importance which are too little noticed. At all times, amid truculent wars ever reviving, there are signs of a conscious effort to prevent war or to mitigate it. Man has never been so ferocious, or so stupid, as to submit to such an evil as war without some kind of effort to prevent it. It is not always easy to read the tokens of his desire and endeavour to obviate war or to diminish its cruelties ; it takes some time to interpret these signs ; but when attention is directed to them they are quite unmistakable. The number of ancient institutions which bear the marks of a design to stand in the way of war, and to provide an alternative to it, is exceedingly great. There are numerous old forms of trial discoverable in a great number of countries and in a great number of races in which, among the ceremonial acts of the parties, you can see evidence of a mimic combat. The Roman *sacra-*

mentum is the best and most familiar instance of this.
What we call a judicial proceeding is obviously taking
the place of a fight.   Another expedient, which is a
good deal misunderstood, is the pecuniary fine which
was imposed sometimes on the individual author of a
homicide, sometimes on his tribe, the Wehr Geld of
the Germans, the Eric fine of the ancient Irish.   I
have seen it represented as evidence of the slight
value attached by these races to human life.   Here
(it is said) is a mere money compensation for killing an enemy.   But this is a misapprehension of the
amount of the punishment inflicted.   If we had
learned that a man who took the life of another was
deprived of the whole of his land we should, I suppose, have been of opinion that the punishment was
at all events not trivial.   But one of the new ideas
which we owe to the ancient Irish law, the Brehon
law, is an adequate conception which we for the
first time gain of the importance to mankind of move-
able property.   *Capitale*, cattle, capital, a long descended term, was the imperatively required imple-
ment for the cultivation of land, at a time when land
was plentiful and perhaps common and undivided.
The necessity imposed on the family or tribe of a man
who had taken a life of paying a portion of this
jealously guarded subject of ownership to another of
the ancient groups was not a slight but an exceedingly heavy penalty.

It is remarkable further that, among the tribal groups of which society was primitively or anciently made up, the observance of good faith seems to have been more strict than among individuals.   There is some evidence of want of respect for sanctity of agreement among individuals, but not so amid tribes. The ancient monuments which are open to us no doubt generally recount victories and defeats, but they also record treaties.   Treaties of great complexity and antiquity are found among the surviving savages. Also we have a glimpse of systems of what would now be called International Law ; that is to say of rules enforced with a regular ceremonial by trained official agents.   Such was the *jus fetiale* of the Romans. And it is to be noted that there are certain departments of this law in which stricter provision seems to have been made than were at the outset found in modern days in what is technically called the Law of Nations ; for example, the extremely express and severe rules which regulate declarations of war.

In modern days the name of International Law has been very much confined to rules laid down by one particular class of writers.   They may be roughly said to begin in the first half of the seventeenth century, and to run three parts through the eighteenth century.   The names which most of us know are first of all that of the great Hugo Grotius, followed by Puffendorf, Leibnitz, Zouch, Selden,

Wolf, Bynkershoek, and Vattel. The list does not absolutely begin with Grotius, nor does it exactly end with Vattel, and indeed as regards the hither end of this series the assumption is still made, and I think not quite fortunately, that the race of law-creating jurists still exists. It is further to be noted that before international law fell into the hands of these writers it had like most other subjects of thought attracted the attention of the Church. There is a whole chapter of the law of nations which is treated of by Roman Catholic theological writers, and a slight difference which distinguishes their use of technical expressions, such for example as 'law of nature' and 'natural law,' occasionally perplexes the student of the system before us.

The rules, however, laid down by the writers I have named and a few others, the nature of their system, and the degree in which it is settled, will occupy much of our time in the present or future courses of lectures. In the first place their system is that conventionally known as International Law; and secondly in them we find, not only the writers at whom Dr. Whewell's implied condemnation is aimed, but the writers whose works acted on the spirit of belligerency like a charm, who did prevent wars and mitigate them, and did something to prepare a time when war should be no more. I said something a few minutes ago of the effect of great agglomerations of countries in terri-

torial empires in producing peace. When the Roman Empire had broken up, after a while the new
European world was long protected against incessant
war by its surviving authority. Its very shadow
gave as much peace as was to be had. The pope
or the emperor, each a continuation of the Cæsars,
served as a court of arbitration and did compose disputes and prevent wars. Too much influence must
not, I have to warn you, be attributed to their
influence. Their sphere was more particularly Italy;
but Ferrari, an historian who has written both in
Italian and French, and who has conceived the
expedient of mapping out Italian history into periods
according to the nature of the revolutions which
occurred in the Italian States, has counted among
these states no less than 7,000 revolutions, each with
a war of its own, small or great. Still the emperor
and the pope, and yet more the pope than the
emperor, were unquestionably, on the whole, makers
of peace ; and sometimes the place of the pope was
taken by a prince of acknowledged sanctity, like
St. Louis of France. But the outbreak of the great
wars of religion, the wars between Catholic and
Protestant, put an end to these pacific influences.
The pope, of course, was necessarily on one side
among the combatants, and on the whole the
emperor was on the same side. Hence it came about
that the great international jurists belonged to the

smaller states and were wholly Protestants.   The
International Law of the Roman Catholic doctors had
fallen into suspicion and finally into disrepute.   A
law with a new sanction was required if states were
to obey it, and this is what the new jurists produced.
The effect was a rapid mitigation of wars and a rapid
decrease in their frequency.

It is very important that we should ask ourselves
what is the true place in legal history of the set of
rules called International Law.   It will be found that
the proper answer to this question involves replies
to several less general questions which are nowadays
put by critical writers, or which spontaneously suggest themselves to the mind of the student, as to the
nature and authority of the famous system before us.
What, then, is its place in the general development of
European jurisprudence ?   We may answer pretty
confidently that its rapid advance to acceptance by
civilised nations was a stage, though a very late stage,
in the diffusion of Roman Law over Europe.   Those
of you who have paid any attention to the history
of law are aware that I have now touched upon a
subject of much interest, and of some difficulty.   In
considerably less than a century, all the ideas of
learned men on the history of Roman Law in the
western world have undergone change.   A hundred
years ago, the virtually universal assumption of
juridical writers was that, when the pressure of in-

vading barbarous races had broken up the territories of the Roman Empire into separate kingdoms, the Roman Law was lost, as the Empire itself was supposed to have been lost.   It was indeed plain that, if this were so, the Roman Law must in some way or other, and at some time or other, have undergone a revival, and this was explained by fables, like the story of the discovery of a copy of Justinian's Pandects at the siege of Amalfi.

More recent learning, learning which on some points is extremely recent, has taught us that many of these assumptions are doubtful and many others are certainly false.   The Roman Empire was never wholly lost, nor the Roman Law either.   The Empire, with Cæsar at the head of it, and with some institutions associated with it which even pointed back to the Republican Roman period, survived to be destroyed by Napoleon Bonaparte, though no doubt it was ever decaying and sinking into a heap of ceremonies, names, and forms.   The Roman Law, on the other hand, was practically everywhere, and its tendency was, not to decay, but to extend its area and enlarge its authority.   The systems of local custom which first established themselves in the new Europe betray a large ingredient of Roman Law in many portions of their structure.   At a later date, writers of treatises professing to set forth the whole, or a definite part, of the institutions of particular

countries, are found to have borrowed considerable
fragments of books which the Romans regarded as of
authority. And then we seem to see a whole flood
of Roman jurisprudence spreading to the ends of
civilised Europe.

No one explanation can be offered of these facts.
In some countries, the Roman Law probably never
ceased to be obeyed, and the foreign element in
its institutions was the barbarous usage. In others
the reverse of this occurred ; the basis, at least
the theoretical basis, of the institutions was barbarous, but the Roman Law, still known to some
classes, was rapidly absorbed. A barbarous system
of law is always scanty, and if it be contiguous to
a larger and more extensive system, the temptation
in practitioners to borrow from this is irresistible.
Only the other day, this process was full in view in
British India. The bulk of the Native Indian law
was extremely narrow. In whole departments of
affairs, no rules were found to settle controversies
which naturally rose up. And the result was that
the bulk of Native Indian law was gradually becoming English through the filtration of rules into it
from the more extensive system by its side. And
this went on, until both the English and the purely
Native law were gradually superseded by the new
Indian Codes. We are not, however, to suppose that
the Roman Law came to be received by European

communities through any process resembling legislation. In the history of law, it is always essential to
keep in mind the fact that legislatures are of very
recent appearance in modern Europe. The earliest
attempt to distinguish clearly between legislative and
executive power, between legislative and executive
action, has been traced to an Italian writer of the
fourteenth century. The powerful bodies from which
many of the legislatures are descended, assemblies of
great men advising and controlling kings, were not
true legislatures themselves. They assisted occasionally in the making of laws, but that was because
law-making was recognised as important business,
and the duty of these Councils, Parliament or States-
General, was to advise the King in all important
business. In truth, far the most influential cause of
the extension of particular laws and of particular
systems of law over new areas was the approval of
them by literate classes, by clergymen and lawyers,
and the acquiescence of the rest of the community
in the opinions of these classes. When then we are
asked by what legislative authority International Law
came to be adopted so as to make it binding on
particular communities, we should rejoin that the
same question must first be put respecting the extension of Roman law and of every other system of law
which, before the era of legislatures, gave proof of
possessing the same power of self-propagation.

A great part, then, of International Law is Roman
Law, spread over Europe by a process exceedingly
like that which, a few centuries earlier, had caused
other portions of Roman Law to filter into the inter-
stices of every European legal system. The Roman
element in International Law belonged, however, to
one special province of the Roman system, that which
the Romans themselves called Natural Law or, by
an alternative name, Jus Gentium. In a book published some years ago on ' Ancient Law ' I made this
remark : ' Setting aside the Treaty Law of Nations,
it is surprising how large a part of the system is made
up of pure Roman law. Wherever there is a doctrine
of the Roman jurisconsults affirmed by them to be in
harmony with the Jus Gentium, the Publicists have
found a reason for borrowing it, however plainly it
may bear the marks of a distinctively Roman origin.'
I must observe, however, that the respect for natural
law as the part of the Roman Law which had most
claims on our reverence did not actually begin with
the international lawyers. The habit of identifying
the Roman law with the Law of Nature, for the purpose of giving it dignity, was of old date in Europe.
When a clergyman or a lawyer of an early age wishes to
quote the Roman Law in a country in which its authority
was not recognised, or in a case to which Roman Law
was not allowed to apply, he calls it ' Natural Law.'
When our Edward III. laid a document before the

Pope for the purpose of establishing his claim to the French throne, and of contending that the descendants of women may succeed to the property or throne of a male ancestor, he spoke of himself as arguing on Natural Law ; though in point of fact the power of women to transmit rights of inheritance to their descendants was pure Roman Law of recent origin, and was not specially connected in any way with the Law of Nature.

But though the founders of the system which lies at the basis of the rules now regulating the concerns of states *inter se* were not the first to describe the Law of Nature and the Law of Nations, Jus Naturæ, Jus Gentium, as the most admirable, the most dignified portion of Roman Law, they speak of it with a precision and a confidence which were altogether new. They look upon it as perfectly determinable if the proper tests be applied, partly on the authority of express texts of Roman Law, partly by a process of inference from a great mass of recorded precedents. Its fitness for international purposes they regard as a discovery of their own, and some writers of their day speak of the system as the new science. No more doubt of its reality seems to have been entertained than (let us say) of the English common law by an English mediæval lawyer. It is sometimes difficult to be quite sure how Grotius and his successors distinguished rules of the Law of Nature from religious

rules prescribed by inspired writers. But that they
did draw a distinction is plain. Grotius's famous
work, the ' De Jure Belli et Pacis,' is in great part
composed of examples supplied by the language and
conduct of heathen statesmen, generals, and sovereigns,
whom he could not have supposed to know anything
of inspired teaching. If we assume him to have
believed that the most humane and virtuous of the
acts and opinions which he quotes were prompted
by an instinct derived from a happier state of the
human race, when it was still more directly shaped
and guided by Divine authority, we should probably
have got as near his conception as possible. As
time has gone on, some parts of this basis of thought
have proved to be no longer tenable. Grotius greatly
overrated the extent of recorded history and, still
more, the accuracy of the record. The very conception from which he started, the conception of a real
and determinable Law of Nature, has not resisted the
application of modern criticism. To each successive
inquirer, the actual childhood of the human race
looks less and less like the picture which the jurists
of the seventeenth century formed of it. It was
excessively inhuman in war; and it was before all
things enamoured of legal technicality in peace. But
nevertheless the system founded on an imaginary
reconstruction of it more and more calmed the fury
of angry belligerency, and supplied a framework to

which more advanced principles of humanity and convenience easily adjusted themselves.

The effects of the ' De Jure Belli et Pacis,' both in respect of its general influence and of the detailed propositions which it laid down, were exceedingly prompt and have proved extremely durable. At about the middle of his reign Louis XIV. of France adopted two measures by which he was thought to have carried the severity of war to the furthest point. He devastated the Palatinate, expressly directing his officers to carry fire and sword into every corner of the province, and he issued a notice to the Dutch, with whom he was at war, that, as soon as the melting of the ice opened the canals, he would grant no more quarter to his Dutch enemies. The devastation of the Palatinate has become a proverb of savageness with all historians, though fifty years earlier it might at most have been passed as a measure of severity, or might even have been defended ; but the proclamation to the Dutch called forth a burst of execration from all Europe, and the threat to refuse quarter was not acted upon. The book of Grotius was making itself felt, and the successors of Grotius assure us that it was his authority which deterred the French king and the French generals from the threatened outrage.

But there is other evidence of the respect paid to the details of his system. Among the most interesting legal products of our day are the Manuals of the usages of war which a great number of civilised states are now issuing to their officers in the field. The Manual prepared for the United States is the oldest of them, but most of them have followed the attempt to form a Code of Land War which was made at the Conference at Brussels in 1874, an attempt which miscarried principally through recollections of the course of the great Franco-German war in 1870–1871. There is very much that is remarkable in all this private codification, as I propose to show in one or two lectures which will follow ; but perhaps the most singular feature of the Manuals is the number of rules adopted in them which have been literally borrowed from the ' De Jure Belli et Pacis,' and specially from its third book. Remembering what Grotius himself says of the condition in which he found the law and usage of war when he began to write of it, and recalling what we learn from historical sources of the wars of succession and the wars of religion, we may well believe Vattel, the Swiss Jurist, a contemporary of the Seven Years' War and of Frederick the Great, when he tells us that what struck him most in the wars of his day was their extreme gentleness ; and of the standard of gentleness proper to be followed in war Vattel was a severe judge.

I here conclude this Introductory Lecture, but there still remain some points of principle which meet us on the threshold of International Law, and which cannot be dismissed absolutely in silence. In my next lecture I propose to consider the binding force of International Law, and with it a question of some gravity on which the judges of England and the legal authorities of the United States do not entertain absolutely identical opinions, and I will state the way in which I venture to think the various shades of difference can be got over. In the succeeding lectures I shall have to consider a few fundamental topics in the system before us, and I hope afterwards to give a sketch, which must be brief on account of the narrow limits of my course, on the law of war by sea and land ; and finally I will endeavour to discharge a part of the duty imposed on me by Dr. Whewell's directions, and to state what measures proposed in our day seem to me to tend to diminish the evils of war and to do something towards extinguishing it among nations.

LECTURE II.

ITS AUTHORITY AND SANCTION.

In the latter portion of the last lecture I endeavoured to establish three propositions, which I hold to be extremely important to the intelligent study of International Law. The first of them was that the process by which International Law obtained authority in a great part of Europe was a late stage of the process by which the Roman Law had also obtained authority over very much the same part of the world. Next, I said that this process had little or no analogy to what is now understood by legislation, but consisted in the reception of a body of doctrine in a mass by specially constituted or trained minds. Lastly, I contended that this doctrine, so spread over Europe, consisted mainly of that part of the Roman Law which the Romans themselves had called Jus Gentium or Jus Naturæ—Law of Nations, or Law of Nature ; terms which had become practicably convertible.

The inquiry into the exact meaning of the phrase

'Law of Nature' belongs to a different department
of juridical study, and I think it will be sufficient
if I briefly summarise the views, themselves considerably condensed, which I published some years
ago in a volume from which I quoted in the last
lecture. Jus Gentium, or Law of Nations, had not,
so I thought, much colour at first of the meaning
which it afterwards acquired. It was probably, I said,
half as a measure of police, and half in furtherance
of commerce, that jurisdiction was first assumed in
disputes in which either foreigners, or a native and a
foreigner, were concerned. In order to obtain some
principles upon which the questions to be adjudicated
on could be settled, the Roman prætor peregrinus
resorted to the expedient of selecting the rules of law
common to Rome and to the different Italian communities in which the immigrants were born. In other
words, he set himself to form a system answering to
the primitive and literal meaning of Jus Gentium, that
is *law common to all nations*. Jus Gentium was in fact
the sum of the common ingredients in the customs of
the old Italian tribes. It was accordingly a collection of rules and principles determined by observation
to be common to the institutions which prevailed
among the various Italian races. Now, it is to be
remembered that every Roman of position who
followed public life was in the course of his official
career not only, so far as his powers went, a statesman,

but specially a general and a judge. Speculation upon legal principles manifestly became common among the Roman aristocracy, and in course of time the question suggested itself what was the essential nature of this Jus Gentium which had at first very possibly been regarded as a mere market law. The answer was shaped by the Greek philosophy, which was a favourite subject of study among the class to which the Roman lawyers belonged. Seen in the light of Stoical doctrine the Law of Nations came to be identified with the Law of Nature ; that is to say, with a number of supposed principles of conduct which man in society obeys simply because he is man. Thus the Law of Nature is simply the Law of Nations seen in the light of a peculiar theory. A passage in the Roman Institutes shows that the expressions were practically convertible. The greatest function of the Law of Nature was discharged in giving birth to modern International Law and the modern Law of War.

I ought to observe that in this account of the matter probably one correction has to be made. Some acute scholars have examined the authorities since I wrote, and they are inclined to think that very anciently there are some instances of the use of Jus Gentium in a wider and something like its modern sense ; that is, law binding on tribes and nations as such. Granting that this is so, still the impression that the

Roman Law contained a system of what would now be called International Law, and that this system was identical with the Law of Nature, had undoubtedly much influence in causing the rules of what the Romans called Natural Law to be engrafted on, and identified with, the modern law of nations. When the older Roman sense of the words died out cannot be confidently ascertained, though of course in a world which was divided between two great rival sovereigns, the Roman Emperor and the King of Persia, there was little room for Law of Nations in the true sense of the words.

When, however, at what period, did this Jus Gentium or Jus Naturæ rise into the dignity which the Roman lawyers give to it ? There is a strong probability that this exaltation was not very ancient, but that it took place during the period, roughly about three hundred years, covered by the so-called Roman Peace. That Peace extended from the time at which the Roman Empire was settled by the success of Augustus over all his enemies to the early years of the third century. The Roman Law transformed a large number of the ideas of a great portion of the world ; but its own transformation from a technical to a plastic system was one of the results of the so-called Roman Peace. If we want to know what war is, we should study what peace is, and see what the human mind is when it is unaffected by war. We

should study the Roman Peace, during which the
existing legal conception of the relation of the sexes
framed itself; during which the Christian Church
was organised, and during which the old Law of
Nations or Nature transformed itself into an ideal
system specially distinguished by simplicity and sym-
metry, and became a standard for the legal institutions of all systems of jurisprudence.

The second proposition for which I argued is one
of very considerable importance.   It was that the Law
of Nations, as framed by the jurists who were its
authors, spread over the world not by legislation, but
by a process of earlier date.   On the appreciation of
this position depends not only the view taken of the
Law of Nature and of the application of International
Law, but also certain practical consequences which
may be momentous ; and at a quite recent date our
country was in danger of adopting an opinion which
would have separated it from the rest of the civilised
world, and from which it could only be saved by
correct ideas on this very point.

In order that you may convince yourselves what
might be the consequences of demanding a legislative sanction, or a sanction derived from an authority
on a level with that of a modern legislature, for the
rules of International Law, I recommend you to com-
pare the view of it taken by the statesmen and jurists
of the United States of America with that to which

this country might have committed itself, and from which it was delivered by the direct intervention of Parliament. The United States are particularly worth examining in regard to the point before us, because they were an instance of a new nation deliberately setting itself to consider what new obligations it had incurred by determining to take rank as a state. Italy is another and a later example, and there have been some others in South America, but all these societies, made up from smaller pre-existing territorial materials, were greatly influenced by the example of the American Federal Union. The doctrines which the United States adopted may be gathered from some very valuable volumes which the American Government has quite recently caused to be published, and to which I will presently call your attention. The systematic American writers on International Law are less instructive on the points which I am going to place before you than these books, because they usually follow the order of topics taken up by older European writers. But I will quote a passage from one of the most careful and sober of writers, Chancellor Kent, and also from a writer who unhappily died the other day, and whose productions were much valued in the United States—Mr. Pomeroy. You will have to recollect that the question at issue between the English and Americans lawyers was less what is the nature of International Law, and how it arose, than the

question how, and to what extent, have its rules become
binding on independent states.   These questions are
often confounded together, or found to be indissoluble,
as will be plain from the extracts which I am about
to read.

There has been a difference of opinion among
writers concerning the foundation of the Law of
Nations.   It has been considered by some as a mere
system of positive institutions, founded upon consent
and usage ; while others have insisted that it was
essentially the same as the Law of Nature, applied to
the conduct of nations, in the character of moral
persons, susceptible of obligations and laws.   We are
not to adopt either of these theories as exclusively
true.   The most useful and practical part of the Law
of Nations is, no doubt, instituted or positive law,
founded on usage, consent, and agreement.   But it
would be improper to separate this law entirely from
natural jurisprudence, and not to consider it as de-
riving much of its force and dignity from the same
principles of right reason, the same views of the
nature and constitution of man, and the same
sanction of Divine revelation, as those from which the
science of morality is deduced.   There is a natural
and a positive Law of Nations.   By the former, every
state, in its relations with other states, is bound to
conduct itself with justice, good faith, and bene-
volence ; and this application of the Law of Nature

has been called by Vattel the necessary Law of
Nations, because nations are bound by the Law of
Nature to observe it ; and it is termed by others the
internal Law of Nations, because it is obligatory upon
them in point of conscience. We ought not, therefore,
to separate the science of public law from that of ethics,
nor encourage the dangerous suggestion that governments are not so strictly bound by the obligations of
truth, justice, and humanity, in relation to other
powers, as they are in the management of their own
local concerns.

States, or bodies politic, are to be considered as
moral persons, having a public will, capable and free
to do right and wrong, inasmuch as they are collections of individuals, each of whom carries with him
into the service of the community the same binding
law of morality and religion which ought to control
his conduct in private life. The Law of Nations is
a complex system, composed of various ingredients.
It consists of general principles of right and justice,
equally suitable to the government of individuals in
a state of natural equality, and to the relations and
conduct of nations ; of a collection of usages, customs,
and opinions, the growth of civilisation and commerce ; and of a code of positive law.

In the absence of these latter regulations, the
intercourse and conduct of nations are to be governed
by principles fairly to be deduced from the rights and

D

duties of nations, and the nature of moral obligation ;
and we have the authority of the lawyers of antiquity,
and of some of the first masters in the modern
school of public law, for placing the moral obligation
of nations and of individuals on similar grounds,
and for considering individual and national morality
as parts of one and the same science. The Law of
Nations, so far as it is founded on the principles of
Natural Law, is equally binding in every age and
upon all mankind. But the Christian nations of
Europe, and their descendants on this side of the
Atlantic, by the vast superiority of their attainments
in arts, and science, and commerce, as well as in
policy and government ; and, above all, by the
brighter light, the more certain truths, and the more
definite sanction which Christianity has communicated to the ethical jurisprudence of the ancients,
have established a Law of Nations peculiar to themselves. They form together a community of nations
united by religion, manners, morals, humanity, and
science, and united also by the mutual advantages
of commercial intercourse, by the habit of forming
alliances and treaties with each other, of interchang-
ing ambassadors, and of studying and recognising
the same writers and systems of public law.

  This Jus Gentium of the Imperial jurisconsults is
identical with the Law of Nature, or Natural Law,
of many modern ethical and juridical writers ; and

both are, in fact, the law of God, made known somewhat dimly to the whole human race at all times,
and set forth with unmistakable certainty and trans-
cendent power in His revealed will.   This is, in truth,
the highest law by which moral beings can. be
governed ; highest in its Lawgiver, who is omni-
potent over each individual man, as well as over
societies and states ; highest in the absolute perfec-
tion of the rules which it contains ; highest in the
absolute cogency of the commands which it utters ;
highest in the absolute obligation of the duties which
it enforces ; highest in the absolute certainty and
irresistible coercive power of the sanctions which it
wields, and which operate upon the deepest spiritual
nature of every human being.

It must be clear to you, I think, that writers who
adhere to these opinions are not likely to trouble
themselves greatly with the question of the original
obligatory force of International Law.   If the Law of
Nations be binding on states considered as moral
beings on account of its derivation from the Law of
Nature or of God, states when in a healthy moral condition will defer to them as individual men do to
the morality of the Ten Commandments.   The whole
question in fact, as laid down by Kent, and with less
moderation by Pomeroy, is a question of ethics, and
all demand of a legislative sanction may be discarded.
But now let us turn to the four volumes of the

American International Digest edited by Dr. Francis Wharton. It is entitled, ' A Digest of the International Law of the United States,' and it consists of documents relating to that subject issued by Presidents and Secretaries of State, of the decisions of Federal Courts, and of the opinions of Attorneys-General. Among the propositions laid down in these volumes you will find the following, all of them accepted by the American Federal Government.

' The law of the United States ought not, if it be avoidable, so to be construed as to infringe on the common principles and usages of nations and the general doctrines of International Law. Even as to municipal matters the law should be so construed as to conform to the Law of Nations, unless the contrary be expressly prescribed. An Act of the Federal Congress ought never to be construed so as to violate the Law of Nations if any other possible construction remains, nor should it be construed to violate neutral rights or to affect neutral commerce, further than is warranted by the Law of Nations as understood in this country.' Again : ' The Law of Nations is part of the Municipal Law of separate states. The intercourse of the United States with foreign nations and the policy in regard to them being placed by the Constitution in the hands of the Federal Government, its decisions upon these subjects are by universally acknowledged principles of International Law obligatory

on everybody.   The Law of Nations, unlike foreign
Municipal Law, does not have to be proved as a fact.
The Law of Nations makes an integral part of the laws
of the land. Every nation, on being received at her
own request into the circle of civilised government,
must understand that she not only attains rights of
sovereignty and the dignity of national character, but
that she binds herself also to the strict and faithful
observance of all those principles, laws, and usages
which have obtained currency amongst civilised states,
and which have for their object the mitigation of the
miseries of war.   International Law is founded upon
natural reason and justice, the opinions of writers of
known wisdom, and the practice of civilised nations.'

Here you see that according to American doctrine
International Law has precedence both of Federal and
of Municipal Law, unless in the exceptional case where
Federal Law has deliberately departed from it.   It is
regarded by the American lawyers as having very
much the same relation to Federal and State Law as
the Federal Constitution has, and this no doubt is the
reason why in so many famous American law books
Constitutional Law and International Law are the
first subjects discussed, International Law on the
whole having precedence of Constitutional Law.

The principle on which these American doctrines
of International Law repose is, I think, tolerably
plain.   The statesmen and jurists of the United

States do not regard International Law as having become binding on their country through the intervention of any legislature. They do not believe it to be of the nature of immemorial usage, 'of which the memory of man runneth not to the contrary.' They look upon its rules as a main part of the conditions on which a state is originally received into the family of civilised nations. This view, though not quite explicitly set forth, does not really differ from that entertained by the founders of International Law, and it is practically that submitted to, and assumed to be a sufficiently solid basis for further inferences, by Governments and lawyers of the civilised sovereign communities of our day. If they put it in another way it would probably be that the state which disclaims the authority of International Law places herself outside the circle of civilised nations.

There is, however, one community which on one occasion went near to dissenting from the American opinion and from the assumptions which it involves. This was our own country, Great Britain. In one celebrated case, only the other day, the English judges, though by a majority of one only, founded their decision on a very different principle, and a special Act of Parliament was required to re-establish the authority of International Law on the footing on which the rest of the world had placed it. The case was one of great importance and interest,

and it was argued before all the English judges in the
Court of Criminal Appeal. It is known as the Queen
v. Keyn, but is more popularly called the ' Franconia '
Case (2 Ex. Div. 63). The ' Franconia,' a German
ship, was commanded by a German subject, Keyn.
On a voyage from Hamburg to the West Indies, when
within two and a half miles from the beach at Dover,
and less than two miles from the head of the Admiralty pier, the ' Franconia,' through the negligence,
as the jury found, of Keyn, ran into the British ship
' Strathclyde,' sank her, and caused the death of one
of her passengers. Keyn was tried for manslaughter,
and was convicted at the Central Criminal Court ; but
the question then arose whether he had committed
an offence within the jurisdiction of English tribunals.

The point on which that question turned was this.
All the writers on International Law agree that some
portion of the coast water of a country is considered
for some purposes to belong to the country the coasts
of which it washes. There is some difference of
opinion between them as to the exact point to which
this territorial water, which is considered as part of
a country's soil, extends. This doctrine, however,
if it were sound, must at some time or other have
been borrowed by the English courts and lawyers
from international authority. Previous to the appearance of International Law, the law followed in

England was different. The great naval judicial authority was then the Admiral of England, whose jurisdiction was over all British subjects and other persons on board British ships on the high seas. If the doctrine of the international jurists prevailed, a change must, at some time or other, have taken place in the law, and the point arose as to whether any such change could be presumed, and by what agency it could have been effected. The judges were very nearly equally divided on the point, which is a fundamental one affecting the whole view to be taken of the authority of International Law in this country. In the end it was decided by the majority of the judges that no sufficient authority was given for the reception in this country of the so-called International doctrine ; but there was no question that this doctrine was the doctrine of the majority of states, and the inconvenience of having one rule for England and another for the rest of the civilised world was palpably so great that Parliament finally stepped in, and in the year 1878 passed what is called the ' Territorial Waters Act,' by which the jurisdiction of the English Courts which had succeeded to the jurisdiction of the Admiral of England was declared to extend according to the International rule to three miles from the coast line of England. In the course of the judgments which were given, which are extremely learned, curious, and interesting, Lord

Coleridge, who was with the minority of the judges, used the following language :

'My brothers Brett and Lindley have shown that by a consensus of writers, without one single authority to the contrary, some poition of the coast waters of a country is considered for some purposes to belong to the country the coasts of which they wash.   I concur in thinking that the discrepancies to be found in these writers as to the precise extent of the coast waters which belong to a country—discrepancies, after all, not serious since the time at least of Grotius —are not material in this question ; because they all agree in the principle that the waters, to some point beyond low-water mark, belong to the respective countries—on grounds of sense if not of necessity, belong to them as territory in sovereignty, or property, exclusively, so that the authority of France or Spain, of Holland or England, is the only authority recog- nised over the coast waters which adjoin these coun- tries.   This is established as solidly as by the very nature of the case any proposition of International Law can be.   Strictly speaking, "International Law " is an inexact expression, and it is apt to mislead if its inexactness is not kept in mind.   Law implies a lawgiver, and a tribunal capable of enforcing it and coercing its transgressors.   But there is no common lawgiver to sovereign states ; and no tribunal has the power to bind them by decrees or coerce them if they transgress. The Law of Nations is that collection of usages which civilised states have agreed to observe in their dealings with one another. What these usages are, whether a particular one has or has not been agreed to, must be matter of evidence. Treaties and acts of state are but evidence of the agreement of nations, and do not in this country at least *per se* bind the tribunals. Neither, certainly, does a consensus of jurists ; but it is evidence of the agreement of nations on international points ; and on such points, when they arise, the English Courts give effect, as part of English law, to such agreement' (p. 153).

Lord Chief Justice Cockburn, on the other hand, after discussing at length the views of thirty writers of different countries and commenting on the difference between them, goes on to remark : 'Can a portion of that which was before high sea have been converted into British territory without any action on the part of the British Government or Legislature —by the mere assertions of writers on public law— or even by the assent of other nations ? And when in support of this position, or of the theory of the three-mile zone in general, the statements of the writers on International Law are relied on, the question may well be asked, upon what authority are these statements founded ? When and in what manner have the nations, who are to be affected by such a rule as these writers, following one another, have laid down, signified their assent to it ?—to say nothing of the difficulty which might be found in saying to which of these conflicting opinions such assent had been given' (p. 202).

It would appear, therefore, from the authorities which I have cited that in the two great English-speaking people of the world, one descended from the other, there prevail two, and possibly three, opinions as to the obligatory force of International Law on individual states.   The lawyers and statesmen of the United States of America regard the acknowledgment of and submission to the international system as duties which devolve on every independent sovereignty through the fact of its being admitted into the circle of civilised Governments.   Among the English judges, Lord Coleridge considers that the assent of a nation is necessary to subject it to International Law, but that in the case of Great Britain and all the other civilised European Powers this assent has been given either by express action or declaration, or at all events by non-dissent.   Lastly, Lord Chief Justice Cockburn, while accepting the view that International Law became binding on states by their assent to it, manifestly thought that this assent must somehow be conveyed by the acquiescing state in its sovereign character, through some public action which its Constitution recognises as legally qualified to adopt a new

law or a new legal doctrine ; that is, in Great Britain
by Act of Parliament or by the formal declaration of a
Court of Justice. The two opinions which I first mentioned, that over and over again propounded in the
American Digest and that of Lord Coleridge, though
the language used is somewhat inexact and in one
case too metaphorical, seem to me to express the
doctrine of the whole civilised world outside Great
Britain, and to conform to the historical explanation
which I will presently place before you. On the
other hand, the opinion of Lord Chief Justice Cockburn, which is one to which English judges, always
busily occupied in interpreting and applying the laws
of this country, are naturally liable, would have caused
the greatest inconvenience if it had been declared to
be part of the law of England. It practically is that
the international rules could only have been imported
into our system by one of the modern processes by
which our institutions are changed. In that case each
separate alleged rule of International Law would have
had to be shown to have been engrafted on our legal
system by the legislation of Parliament, by the alternative legislation, within certain limits, of the English
Courts, or by the conformity of the rule with some
provable usage. For a simple rule a most complicated rule would have been substituted.

The point immediately before the English Court
of Criminal Appeal can never arise again since the

passing of the Territorial Waters Act ; but it is conceivable, if not likely, that we have not heard the last
of the more general question of principle. I may say
that it seems to me that the solution of the difficulty
can only be supplied by the historical method. As I
have asserted many times, these systems of law have
not always been extended over the countries in which
they are found prevailing by what we call legislation.
In more ancient times, and to a great extent even at
this day, in that Eastern portion of the world in
which so much of the usages of earlier mankind still
survive, systems of religion and systems of morals,
generally drawing with them some system of laws,
gain currency by their own moral influence ; certain
minds being naturally predisposed to receive them
acquiesce in them even with enthusiasm. Mr.
Justice Stephen, in the controversial work which he
calls ' Liberty, Equality, and Fraternity,' has an
eloquent passage on the subject. ' The sources of
religion lie hid from us. All that we know is, that
now and again in the course of ages some one sets to
music the tune which is haunting millions of ears. It
is caught up here and there, and repeated till the
chorus is thundered out by a body of singers able to
drown all discords and to force the vast unmusical
mass to listen to them. Such results as these come
not by observation, but when they do come they carry
away as with a flood and hurry in their own direc-

tion all the laws and customs of those whom they affect.' What is here said of religion, is true to a certain extent of morality. In the East a body of new moral ideas is sure in time to produce a string of legal rules ; and it is said by those who know India and its natives well that the production of what for want of a better name we must call a Code is a favourite occupation with learned and active minds, though of course in a country which nowadays follows to a great extent the morality (though not the faith) of Christian Europe, and receives new laws from a regularly constituted Legislature, the enthusiasm for new moral doctrines is ever growing feebler and the demand for legal rules accommodated to them is becoming less. Now, International Law was a Code in the same sense in which many Eastern collections of rules were Codes. It was founded on a new morality, that which had been discovered in the supposed Law of Nature, and in some minds it excited unbounded enthusiasm.

The same process had previously been followed in Europe as regards Roman Civil Law. We may not quite understand the admiration which the technical part of the Roman Law inspired, but of the fact there is no doubt. This process by which laws extended themselves had not quite died out when the international jurists appeared, and in point of fact their system of rules was received by the world very

much as a system of law founded on morals is
received to this day in the East. No doubt it fell on
soil prepared for it. The literate classes, the scholars,
great parts of the clergy, and the sovereigns and
statesmen of Europe accepted it, and the result was
an instant decay of the worst atrocities of war. Indeed,
it is only necessary to look at the earliest authorities
on International Law, in the ' De Jure Belli et Pacis '
of Grotius for example, to see that the Law of Nations
is essentially a moral and, to some extent a religious,
system. The appeal of Grotius is almost as frequent
to morals and religion as to precedent, and no doubt
it is these portions of the book, which to us have
become almost commonplace or which seem irrelevant, which gained for it much of the authority which
it ultimately obtained.

The bulk of these lectures will consist of an
account, as summary as I can make it, of such portions of the International system as appear to me to
be reasonably settled ; but before I proceed to this
portion of my course, I think I ought to say something on some modern criticisms of the basis of
International Law which have made their appearance
quite recently, and which I think have a tendency to
multiply. The criticisms to which I refer appear to
me to be a singular proof of the great authority which
in our day has been obtained by the treatise of John
Austin on the Province of Jurisprudence. They are

in fact to a considerable extent a re-statement of his
positions. The scope of Austin's undertaking in this
classical work is often nowadays exaggerated. He
attempted, by analysis of the various conceptions
which law in its various senses includes, to select
one sense of law in which legal generalisations were
possible. His ultimate object appears to have been
to effect a scientific rearrangement of law as a Code.
Little unfortunately has been done at present, save
perhaps in the German Empire and in India, to carry
out this object ; but no doubt Austin did do something
towards the ultimate codification of positive law by
confining his investigation to the various subordinate
conceptions which make up law as so understood. As
probably many of you know, his fundamental assertion is that in every country there is some portion of
the community which can force the rest to do exactly
what it pleases. This is called by him the ' Sovereign,'
a word on which it is necessary as soon as possible
to observe that it is here taken in a different sense
from that in which it is employed by the classical
writers on International Law. From Austin's point
of view International Law resembled morality more
than law ; it was chiefly enforced by disapprobation
of acts committed in violation of it ; it could not be
resolved into the command of any sovereign.

In my next lecture, I shall contrast this word
' Sovereignty ' as used by Austin and the so-called

school of analytical jurists with its use in International
Law, and specially consider the rights over land and
water which are asserted by international lawyers to
arise logically from the conception of Sovereignty.

In my first lecture I spoke of the criticisms on
International Law conducted by John Austin in his
' Province of Jurisprudence Determined' as very interesting and quite innocuous; but the results are sometimes so stated as if they showed that Austin had intended to diminish, and had succeeded in diminishing,
the dignity or imperative force of International Law.
An observation here must be made that one sense of law
is just as good and dignified as another, if it be only
consistently used.   In philosophy the commonest sense
of law is that in which it is used by such writers as the
author of the book called ' The Reign of Law.'   No
term can be more dignified or more valuable than 'law'
as thus employed.   What we have to do, is to keep this
meaning of law separate in our minds from law in
other senses.   It is very convenient, when the main
subject of thought is positive law, that we should
remember that International Law has but slender
connection with it, and that it has less analogy to
the laws which are the commands of sovereigns than
to rules of conduct, which, whatever be their origin,
are to a very great extent enforced by the disapprobation which attends their neglect.   What is most
important to recollect are the points of connection

E

which *do* exist between International Law and positive law.

Here one cannot but remark that a serious mistake as to human nature is becoming common in our day. Austin resolved law into the command of a sovereign addressed to a subject, and always enforced by a sanction or penalty which created an imperative duty. The most important ingredient brought out by this analysis is the sanction. Austin has shown, though not without some straining of language, that the sanction is found everywhere in positive law, civil and criminal. This is, in fact, the great feat which he performed, but some of his disciples seem to me to draw the inference from his language that men always obey rules from fear of punishment. As a matter of fact this is quite untrue, for the largest number of rules which men obey are obeyed unconsciously from a mere habit of mind. Men do sometimes obey rules for fear of the punishment which will be inflicted if they are violated, but, compared with the mass of men in each community, this class is but small—probably, it is substantially confined to what are called the criminal classes—and for one man who refrains from stealing or murdering because he fears the penalty there must be hundreds or thousands who refrain without a thought on the subject. A vast variety of causes may have produced this habit of mind. Early teaching certainly has a great deal to do with it ;

religious opinion has a great deal to do with it; and it is very possible, and indeed probable, that in a vast number of cases it is an inherited sentiment springing from the enforcement of law by states, and the organs of states, during long ages. Unfortunately it has been shown in our day that the mental habit, so far as regards positive civil and criminal law, may be easily destroyed by connivance at violations of rule; and this is some evidence of its having a long descent from penal law once sternly enforced.

What we have to notice is, that the founders of International Law, though they did not create a sanction, created a law-abiding sentiment. They diffused among sovereigns, and the literate classes in communities, a strong repugnance to the neglect or breach of certain rules regulating the relations and actions of states. They did this, not by threatening punishments, but by the alternative and older method, long known in Europe and Asia, of creating a strong approval of a certain body of rules. It is quite true that some of the reasons given by Grotius for International Law would not now commend themselves if they were presented to the mind for the first time; but it does not do to look too far back into the origins of law for the reasons of its establishment. Much of the beginnings of English Law is to be found in the Year Books; but it would not be too harsh to say that some of the reasons given for rules now received, which are to be found in the Year Books, are mixed with a great deal of sheer nonsense. The original reasons for the International rules are possibly to some extent nonsense : they often seem to us commonplace, they are often rhetorical, they are often entangled with obsolete theories of morals or deductions from irrelevant precedents, and on the other hand they often assume a power of discerning what the Divine pleasure is on a particular subject which the ideas of the present day would not admit. As to their expediency, that has to be decided by experience, and experience has, on the whole, pronounced decisively in their favour.

There are, however, at the same time some real defects in International Law which are traceable to the difference between that law and positive law, and the absence of mechanism by which positive law is developed. International Law was not declared by a Legislature, and it still suffers from want of a regular Legislature to improve and to develop it. It is still developed by the antiquated method of writer commenting on writer, no security being nowadays taken for the competence or authority of the writer except vague opinion. There are really writers who through confusedness, or through natural prejudice, are open to the implied censure of Dr. Whewell that they have rather encouraged than diminished the risk and the evils of war. International Law suffers also from the absence of any method of authoritatively declaring its tenor on some of its branches, and above all from the absence of any method of enforcing its rules short of war or fear of war. All these are real and often formidable drawbacks on the usefulness of International Law, and no teacher of International Law can neglect them. Before the end of this course, though not quite immediately, I propose to examine them, and to consider whether the growing experience of civilised mankind points to any new remedies or better means of enforcing old ones.

LECTURE III.

STATE SOVEREIGNTY.

I now propose to occupy you with a group of questions arising out of a subject of much interest and magnitude—the Sovereignty of states over land and water. I will first quote a definition of Sovereignty which would fairly, I think, satisfy the jurists of the present day. It is taken from an excellent book by the late Mr. Montague Bernard, of which the title is, ' The Neutrality of Great Britain during the American Civil War.' The definition is primarily a definition of a Sovereign State. ' By a Sovereign State,' says Mr. Bernard, ' we mean a Community or number of persons permanently organised under a Sovereign Government of their own, and by a Sovereign Government we mean a Government, however constituted, which exercises the power of making and enforcing law within a Community, and is not itself subject to any superior Government. These two factors, the one positive, the other negative, the exercise of power and the absence of superior control, compose the notion of Sovereignty and are essential to it.'

It is necessary to observe that the conception of Sovereignty went through several changes before it became capable of this description. The view of Sovereignty taken by the earliest international jurists in the sixteenth and seventeenth centuries appears to me to be taken from Roman Law. It is at bottom *dominium*—dominion, ownership. We should not be far wrong in saying that these writers regard the civilised world as a space of soil divided between a number of Roman proprietors ; much of their language is taken directly from Roman Law ; and, as usual, it is taken particularly from those rules of the Roman system which the Romans themselves believed to be identical with the rules of the Law of Nature. Many fundamental principles are explained by this view. Thus all States, in International Law, are regarded as equal. As a writer of the last century said, Russia is regarded as is Geneva ; and in the same way so would a set of Roman owners be regarded as equal before the law. Again, International Law pays regard to Sovereigns only, it does not regard any other part of the community any more than a Roman tribunal would regard the slaves and freedmen of a Roman estate. I think too that these jurists, on the whole, regard the Sovereign as an individual man. It is true that so many of them belonged to the few republics then existing, and specially to the United Provinces of the Netherlands, that they were of course aware of the

necessity of occasionally contemplating the Sovereign
as a corporation ; but on the whole the view which
is at the basis of their conception is that the Sovereign
is an individual ; and sovereigns are regarded by these
lawyers as absolute and not merely paramount owners
of the states which they govern.   They do not look
below the existing Prince or Ruler, who had been
originally a man exercising despotic power.   Further,
Sovereignty is at this date always associated with a
definite portion of the earth's surface.

But Sovereignty, or what corresponded in ancient
time most nearly to it, was not primitively associated
with all these ideas ; they took the place of other
ideas of older date.   Thus Sovereignty was not always
territorial ; it was not always associated with a definite
portion of the earth's surface.   I have pointed out,
in the work from which I have several times quoted,
that the older ideas are reflected in the titles of the
earliest Monarchs in Western Europe.   These were
Rex Anglorum, Rex Francorum, Rex Scotorum—King
of the English, King of the Franks, King of the
Scots.   And one of the most pathetic figures in
history is still always known to us as the 'Queen
of Scots.'   Evidently the fundamental conception was
that the territory belonged to the Tribe, and that the
Sovereign was Sovereign of the Tribe.   The fact is
that the feudalisation of Europe had to be completed
before it was possible that Sovereignty could be

associated with a definite portion of soil. The investigation of the process which we call feudalisation does not belong to this branch of Historical Jurisprudence : but there is no doubt that in the long run Sovereignty came always to be associated with the last stage of this process. The lawyers on the whole regard Sovereignty as the Sovereignty exercised by individuals, and the result was extremely important to International Law, for the assumed individuality of sovereigns enabled its founders to regard states as moral beings bound by moral rules. If the units of the International system had continued to be what they apparently were at first, tribes or collections of men, it is doubtful whether that system could have been constructed, and at all events, whether it could have taken its actual present form.

Some of the words in Mr. Bernard's definition reflect a much later influence upon law—e.g. that of Mr. John Austin. He gives to the position that a sovereign Government cannot be controlled by another, an importance which can hardly be said to belong to it in International Law. The position is, in fact, indispensable in Austin's system. There is, in his view, an all-powerful portion of every community which can do what it pleases as regards the rest, and this all-powerful portion or Sovereign is the author of law. No objection can be taken to it from the view of Austin's theory ; but it should be always

carefully remembered in our branch of jurisprudence
that Mr. John Austin's definition of Sovereignty is
not that of International Law, though in almost all
the very modern treatises which have dealt with this
subject some confusion between the two is observable.
It is necessary to the Austinian theory that the all-
powerful portion of the community which make laws
should not be divisible, that it should not share its
power with anybody else, and Austin himself speaks
with some contempt of the semi-sovereign or demi-
sovereign states which are recognised by the classical
writers on International Law.   But this indivisibility
of Sovereignty, though it belongs to Austin's system,
does not belong to International Law.   The powers
of sovereigns are a bundle or collection of powers,
and they may be separated one from another.   Thus
a ruler may administer civil and criminal justice, may
make laws for his subjects and for his territory, may
exercise power over life and death, and may levy
taxes and dues, but nevertheless he may be debarred
from making war and peace, and from having foreign
relations with any authority outside his territory.
This in point of fact is the exact condition of the
native princes of India ; and states of this kind are
at the present moment rising in all the more barbarous portions of the world.   In the protectorates
which Germany, France, Italy, and Spain have established in the Australasian seas and on the coast of

Africa, there is no attempt made to annex the land or to found a colony in the old sense of the word, but the local tribes are forbidden all foreign relations except those permitted by the protecting state. As was the declared intention of the most powerful founder of protectorates of this kind, Prince Bismarck, if they were to resemble anything they were to resemble India under the government of the East India Company.

As a matter of fact nearly all the modern writers on International Law do divide the rights flowing from the Sovereignty of states into groups. Their distribution of those rights is not uniform, and some of their divisions are more defensible than others. Grotius divided the law of which he wrote, as is known from the title of his book, into law of war and law of peace; and writers of our day, following this distribution, but falling into an error into which Grotius did not fall, classify all the rights of states as rights of war and rights of peace. Some modern publicists make a more general division into two classes ; first, primary rights or absolute rights, and in the second place conditional or hypothetical rights; the first being the rights to which a state is entitled as an independent moral body, or in other words that to which it is entitled during peace ; the conditional rights being those to which it is entitled when placed in special circumstances, the special circumstances

contemplated being war. The subject of rights and
duties, arising in a condition of war, will be taken up
at a different point of this course, and to-day we will
confine ourselves to the absolute or primary rights,
those which a state possesses during peace. I observe in modern writers a tendency so to state this
part of the law, and so to argue, as to suggest that
these absolute rights are nothing more than those
which may be logically inferred from the mere fact
that a state has existence. This is very simply put
in the account of the same class of rights which is
given by the author of a valuable work on International Law, Mr. Hall. He says : ' Under the conditions of state life the right to continue and develop
existence gives to a state other classes of rights.
These are: first, to organise itself in such manner as
it may choose ; secondly, to do within its dominions
whatever acts it may think calculated to render it
prosperous and strong ; thirdly, to occupy unappropriated territory and to incorporate new provinces
with the free consent of the inhabitants, provided that
the rights of another state over any such province
are not violated by its incorporation. Thus with
regard to the first power or right which is alleged to
reside, by the nature of the case, in a sovereign
state, the power of organising itself in such a manner
as it may choose, it follows that such a state may
place itself under any form of government that it

wishes, and may frame its social institutions upon
any model. To foreign states, the political or social
doctrines which may be exemplified in it, or which
may spread from it, are legally immaterial.'

This is correct law, and in our day I do not doubt
that to most minds it would seem plain that, the condition of Sovereignty being taken for granted, these
rights so stated follow. But, as a matter of fact, confining ourselves to this branch of state powers, none
have been more violently denied or disputed ; and if
they were preserved it is far less owing to their logical
connection with the definition of state Sovereignty,
than from the fact that, from the very first, the position that they exist has been plainly stated by the
international lawyers. And the fact that these rights
have been preserved is a signal tribute to the importance of International Law. It happens that the
long peace which extended from 1815 to 1854 was,
both at its beginning and at its end, all but broken
up by the denial of these simple rights of which I
have been speaking. The pacification of the Continent, after the overthrow of the French Empire, was
succeeded by a series of movements instituted by
communities for the purpose of obtaining Constitutions ; that is, for guarding against being remitted
to the same condition of despotic rule in which the
French Revolution had found them. All these Constitutions had for their object the limitation of the

powers of the King. Perhaps the most democratic
of them was the one known as the Spanish Constitution of 1812. When in fact the Spanish Cortes
at Cadiz framed this Constitution, Ferdinand, the
King of Spain, was in the hands of the French ; and
therefore the Spanish Constitution-makers had to
contemplate a Constitution suitable to a country from
which the King would be, perhaps, permanently ab-
sent. Naturally, therefore, the powers of the King were
in this Constitution reduced to very little. The
King of Spain, on his return from imprisonment,
denounced this Constitution, but it obtained great
favour in certain parts of Europe, and in 1820 the
Neapolitans, after a revolution, compelled their King
to grant a Constitution which was a copy of it.
Much dismay was caused to the Continental Powers
which retained their despotisms, and the Congresses
of Laybach and Troppau assembled to consider the
danger of the spread of what were then known as
' French principles ' from Naples to the rest of
Europe. It was finally determined that the Nea-
politan Constitution should be modified, and that
compulsion should be put on the not very reluctant
King by the arms of Austria. Great Britain, however, protested against the decision. Soon afterwards
the Constitution of 1812 was adopted after a military
rising in Spain itself. This led to the assemblage of
the Congress of Verona and to the restoration of the

Spanish despotism, the compulsion on this occasion being put upon Spain by France.

Before, however, the European peace finally broke up, the current had turned in the other direction ; and Great Britain, whose foreign affairs were now directed by Lord Palmerston, employed its influence to assist states which desired to obtain Constitutions. In addition to the desire for popular government the spirit of nationality had now come into play ; and the ultimate result was the intervention of Napoleon III. in Italy and the destruction of the Italian despotisms. Therefore all the Powers in Europe, during the peace, did in turn act upon principles from which the inference might be drawn that they denied the right of a state under certain circumstances to adopt what political Constitution it pleases ; nevertheless this rule of law in the long run prevailed ; nor can there be the slightest question that it is of the greatest value. Of all rules of public law it is the one which does most to prevent the whole of the civilised world being brought under an iron-bound theory of government. It enables theories of government to be tested by experiment in several states, and prevents any one of them from overwhelming the rest whether in the name of order or in the name of freedom.

I pass now to the second of the rules which I have quoted from Mr. Hall. Every sovereign state is entitled to do, within its dominions, whatever acts it may think calculated to render it prosperous and strong. Two consequences follow from this position. A state may take what measures it pleases for its own defence ; and a state may adopt whatever commercial system it thinks most likely to promote its prosperity. That a state has these powers is not now denied, and would not, I think, be disputed ; but nevertheless if the existence of these rights had not now for two centuries been affirmed by International Law, I think they would have turned out to be full of pretexts for war. Even at this moment the patience of states is hardly tried by the way in which their neighbours act upon the principle. Take France and Germany. Rarely in the history of the world have there been such achievements of military engineering as are exemplified in the fortresses which line the long border of the two countries. Every one of those fortresses is just as available for attack as for defence ; and knowing what men are, it is really wonderful that no complaint has at present been made of the mere fact of their construction. Take again two dependencies of European countries, which are really great countries standing on a footing of their own—British India and Asiatic Russia. These are not countries in which fortresses are, or are likely to be, constructed in any large number. The conditions of climate and other difficulties render them defences of no great value ; but either Power is

engaged at vast outlay in creating a system of railways within its own countries ; and we can see
even now that any fresh railway constructed within
the border of the one country gives rise at least for
criticism and private complaint on the part of the
other. I do not think we can doubt that if International Law had not been perfectly clear and precise
on the subject of these rights, alleged to flow from the
Sovereignty of states, they would conduce to every
variety of complaint followed by every variety of
war. What really enables states to exercise their
Sovereignty in this way is nothing but the legal rule
itself.

So also with regard to commercial systems. They
differ enormously in contiguous communities. There
is no question that of old the English Navigation
Laws were bitterly disliked by a great part of Europe ;
and now there is a standing difference between a
number of communities on the subject of Free Trade
and Protection, and but for the rule affirming the
unrestricted right to adopt such commercial system
as a country pleases, this difference of economical
opinion would undoubtedly be most dangerous. As
the law stands, a state may directly and deliberately
legislate against the particular industries of another ;
and so far as we are concerned we have so fully
acquiesced in this principle that we allow our colonies
to exercise the privileges once grudgingly conceded

F

to independent states, and to exclude our manufactures by prohibitory fiscal provisions.

The third of Mr. Hall's rules states that a sovereign state has an unlimited power to occupy unappropriated territory. Here is a very great question, which was the fertile source of quarrel in the seventeenth and eighteenth centuries, and which perhaps may assume a new importance in the twentieth. The discovery of the American continent and the growth of maritime adventure gave fresh interest to a subject which had been left in neglected obscurity, and the rising international system was not at first ready with rules to meet it. The first tendency of International Law was to attribute an exaggerated importance to priority of discovery. It was thought by the earlier jurists to be the same thing in principle as the Roman Inventio, the form of occupation by which under the Law of Nature property was acquired in a valuable object, such as a jewel, belonging to nobody. But in our days prior discovery, though still held in considerable respect, is not universally held to give an exclusive title. The United States indeed have not unreservedly agreed to the degradation of first discovery from its old consideration. In 1843 that Government protested against the ground taken by the British Foreign Office that a discovery made by a private individual, in the prosecution of a private enterprise, gives no international right. But the

American Secretary of State in the same despatch admitted it to be a point not yet settled by the usage of nations, how far discovery of a territory which is either unsettled or settled only by savages gives a right to it. (Wharton, i. 5.)   But this inconvenience of resting rights upon mere discovery has caused more distinct forms of occupation or annexation to be preferred to it.   Nearly all titles of discovery are of old date, and many of these are matters of historical dispute ; while at the same time the world is so well known that new titles of discovery are rare.   On the whole, some kind of formal annexation of new territory is now regarded as the best source of title.   It is still allowed that prior discovery, if established, may give legal importance to acts and signs otherwise ambiguous or without validity.   A cairn of stones, a flagstaff or the remains of one, may mean little or nothing if found on a desolate coast ; but if it can be shown to have been put up by the first discoverers, it may obtain great significance and importance.   All discovery is now disregarded, unless it be followed by acts showing an intention to hold the country as your own, the most conclusive of these acts being the planting upon it some civil or military settlement.

A great distinction is now drawn between appropriators of new territory who are furnished with a general or special authority to effect the annexation, and appropriators who have no such

authority.   If the state to which the commissioned
appropriator belongs should afterwards ratify the
appropriation, a good international title would be
acquired by it, and so also if authority to appropriate
on behalf of the state had been originally given.   In
the case of an · uncommissioned navigator, something
more than a mere formal assumption of possession
is required.   For example, if a body of adventurers
establish themselves in a previously unappropriated
country, declaring it at the same time to belong to
the state of which they are subjects, this state may
ratify their act and declaration, and the title is made
complete ; but if an uncommissioned navigator takes
possession of a new country in the name of his
Sovereign, and then sails away without forming a
settlement, the modern doctrine is that this originally
imperfect title cannot afterwards be completed by
ratification, and is liable meanwhile to be set aside by
the independent acts of other sovereigns.

LECTURE IV.

TERRITORIAL RIGHTS OF SOVEREIGNTY.

ALL the department of International Law with which I was occupied at the close of my last lecture, the acquisition by a State of unappropriated territory, has been much influenced by the Roman Law. What takes place may still be described by the Roman phrase *occupatio*. The fundamental rule is the same in the original and in the derivative system. In order that new lands may be appropriated, there must be physical contact with them, or physical contact resumable at pleasure, coupled with an intention to hold them as your own.

The leading precedent in such cases is the controversy as to the status of the Oregon territory and as to the mode in which that status arose. You will find it set forth at some length in all the modern international treatises, and more particularly in those of American writers. No dispute more nearly gave rise to a war. The interests at first at stake seemed to be merely those of competing fur companies ;

but this impression has not been justified by the
event. The whole position of the territories in dispute
has been changed by the construction of two great
railways. The Northern Pacific Railway has opened
up the fertile and wealthy lands which were claimed by
the Americans on the south, while on the north the
lands claimed by Great Britain include the Canadian
province of British Columbia, which has been practically incorporated with the Canadian Dominion by
the construction of the Canadian Pacific Railway. I
should perhaps add that the facts in controversy were
not altogether plain ; but it is generally admitted that
Captain Gray, from whom the Americans claimed
title, was the uncommissioned agent of a fur company,
while Captain Vancouver, upon whose discoveries
the English claim was based, though he assumed
possession of the territory for Great Britain, never
took this step till he heard of Gray's observation.
This, after what I have said of the principles, may
serve to show the difficulties of the question at issue.
It was most wisely settled by a compromise embodied
in the Treaty of Washington.

Here let me observe that one great question constantly arises upon the appropriation of territory by
discovery or by occupation : what area of land is
affected by the necessary acts when they are properly
completed ? Settlements are usually first established
upon coasts, and behind them stretch long spaces of

unoccupied territory, from access to which other nations may be cut off by the appropriation of the shore lands, and which, with reference to a population creeping inwards from the sea, must be looked upon as more or less attendant on the coast. What then in this case is involved in the occupation of a given portion of shore ? It seems to be a settled usage that the interior limit shall not extend further than the crest of the watershed. It is also generally admitted, on the other hand, that the occupation of the coast carries with it a right to the whole territory drained by the rivers which empty their waters within its line ; but the admission of this right is perhaps accompanied by the tacit reservation that the extent of coast must bear some reasonable proportion to the territory which is claimed in virtue of its possession.

I said before that the proceedings of several European Powers give us reason to think that questions with regard to Sovereignty over new countries acquired by occupation may again arise, though possibly not in the present century. It is to be observed, however, that hitherto the title, which has been put forward to lands assumed by Germany and France, by Spain and Italy, has very generally been made to rest upon the consent of the native indigenous community occupying them, or of some sort of Government to which they are in the habit of submitting. The question as to the degree in which the occupation of

new land by a savage or barbarous tribe would bar
occupation by civilised settlers is one of considerable
antiquity and of much difficulty, and the way in which
it has been treated has not been generally thought to
reflect credit on civilised explorers or the states to
which they belonged. There is no doubt that international practice started with the assumption that
the native indigenous title might be neglected on the
ground that the inhabitants found in the discovered
countries were heathen. Roman Catholic explorers
and their sovereigns were satisfied with admitting
that it was the duty of states taking possession of
new territory to convert the inhabitants to the Roman
Catholic form of Christianity. The attempts of the
Spanish Government to Christianise the Indians of
Mexico and South America appear to have been quite
honest, and the subsequent sufferings of the aborigines
seem to be attributable to the civil institutions introduced from Spain. In Spain, as in all continental
European countries, at the day of Columbus and
Cortez there existed the *corvée* or obligation to labour
gratuitously for the State on roads and other public
works ; and the *corvée* was transplanted to the new
American dependencies. There was also in the
mining provinces of Northern Spain a considerable population who were bound to work at mining
operations for the benefit of the proprietors, and
whose status very nearly approached that of the slave.

This quasi-servile status was more widely extended, and was even found in Scotland at the beginning of the last century.   It was therefore hardly surprising that it was introduced into Spanish America, North and South, where it brought about frightful cruelties. Queen Isabella of Castile appears to have been sincerely anxious to abate the cruelty of the Spanish forced labour ; but she was assured by the missionaries that, when released from the obligations of cultivation and mining, the timid natives retreated into the wilds from the company of the Spaniards and lost their Christianity.   Many of you must be aware that the origin of negro slavery in South America has been traced to the substitution of a hardier race for the weakly native Indians, who were dying in multitudes,   Perhaps it is only just to remark that, after nearly four centuries, the ill-reputed Spanish experiments have in the long run brought about a nearer assimilation of the white and coloured races than has been seen in any other part of the world. There are some Spanish American Republics in which the whole community is virtually of Indian extraction and colour.

In North America, where the discoverers or new colonists were chiefly English, the Indians inhabiting that continent were compared almost universally to the Canaanites of the Old Testament, and their relation to the colonists was regarded as naturally one

of war almost by Divine ordinance. This view was
first dissented from by an English sect to whom
many experiments in the practical application of
humanity are due—the Quakers ; and the agree-
ments made with the Indians of Pennsylvania by
William Penn satisfied the consciences of those
whom he represented. Nay, further observation
has shown a very decided tendency in the United
States to admit that the land necessary for their
subsistence should not be taken away from the
North American Indians unless in some form or
other sufficient provision be made for their subsistence by agriculture or by hunting. The purely
legal doctrine is this : a very famous American judge,
who did more than any other man to shape the
early jurisdiction of the Supreme Court of the
United States, laid down that the British title to
American territory, which the Federal Government
inherited, excluded the American Indians from all
rights except the right of occupancy, and gave the
Federal Government the power of extinguishing this
right of occupancy by conquest or purchase. But
the admission that enough land must be left for the
subsistence of all savage natives is now generally
made by all proprietors of new territory. As a rule,
however, at the present moment the tribes or communities found on the lands which the European
states have taken possession of, have passed the stage

which the American Indians were in when Europeans first came into contact with them.   Prince Bismarck has expressly declared that he regards the German annexations as following the example of the British East India Company.   Here it is assumed that some organised community is found in possession of the land. After the annexation they retain whatever rights they possessed before, save only the right of having foreign relations with anybody they please.

Up to this point I have been speaking of the jurisdiction and authority claimed by sovereign states over certain definite portions of the earth's surface. The narrow limits of my course forbid my exhausting what is a very extensive subject.   It will be more convenient, I think, that I should leave the remaining topics contained in the subject of Sovereignty over land, and that I should pass on to Sovereignty over water, treating it very briefly.   As before, I merely note points of interest and difficulty which occur as I proceed.   States in fact are in the habit of exercising or claiming sovereign authority over portions of the sea, over lakes and rivers, and over certain vessels belonging to them or to their subjects when lying in the water of the high seas or in water over which they exercise or claim jurisdiction.

The first branch of our inquiry brings us to what, at the birth of International Law, was one of the most bitterly disputed of all questions, the

question of the *mare clausum* and the *mare liberum*—
sea under the dominion of a particular Power or sea
open to all—names identified with the great reputa-
tions of Grotius and Selden. In all probability the
question would not have arisen but for the dictum of
the Institutional Roman writers that the sea was by
nature common property. And the moot point was
whether there was anything in nature, whatever that
word might have meant, which either pointed to the
community of the sea or of rivers, and also what did
history show to have been the actual practice of
mankind, and whether it pointed in any definite way
to a general sense of mankind on the subject. We
do not know exactly what was in the mind of a
Roman lawyer when he spoke of nature. Nor is it
easy for us to form even a speculative opinion as to
what can have been the actual condition of the sea
in those primitive ages somehow associated with the
conception of nature. The slender evidence before
us seems to suggest that the sea at first was common only in the sense of being universally open to
depredation. The sea of early Greek literature
appears to have swarmed with pirates. But there is
older evidence. There are some Egyptian inscriptions
which appear to speak of piratical leagues formed
among the small Mediterranean states for making
descent on weak and wealthy maritime communities.
There are some of the names recorded which may be

identified with the ancient appellations of tribes subsequently famous ; and one cannot avoid the suspicion that the famous war of Troy arose from an expedition of this kind, whatever other pretexts for it there may have been.   Whatever jurisdiction may have been asserted probably did not spring from any-thing which may be called nature, but was perhaps a security against piracy.   At all events this is certain, that the earliest development of Maritime Law seems to have consisted in a movement from *mare liberum*, whatever that may have meant, to *mare clausum*—from navigation in waters over which nobody claimed authority, to waters under the control of a separate sovereign.   The closing of seas meant delivery from violent depredation at the cost or by the exertion of some power or powers stronger than the rest.   No doubt Sovereignty over water began as a benefit to all navigators, and it ended in taking the form of pro-tection.   Mr. W. E. Hall, in a very interesting chapter of his volume (Part ii. 2), has shown that Inter-national Law, in the modern sense of the words, began in a general system of *mare clausum* ; the Adriatic, the Gulf of Genoa, the North Sea, and the Baltic, were all closed and were under authority, and England claimed to have precedence and to exercise jurisdiction of various kinds from the North Sea and the parts of the Atlantic adjoining Scotland and Ireland southwards to the Bay of Biscay.   In all

these waters the omission to lower the flag to a
British ship would have been followed by a cannon
shot.   Thenceforward the progress of maritime
jurisdiction was reversed—from *mare clausum* to *mare
liberum*.   And the Sovereignty allowed by International Law over portions of the sea is in fact a
decayed and contracted remnant of the authority
once allowed to particular states over a great part of
the known sea and ocean.

The causes which threw open a large number of
maria clausa are not obscure.   In the first place
there was the opinion of some of the most respected
and authoritative of the founders of International
Law.   For example, the strong opinion of Grotius,
perhaps the most reverenced of all these writers, that
the proper doctrine was that of the *mare liberum*.
Next, and more especially, this opening of seas was
brought about by the discovery of America and the
passage round the Cape of Good Hope.   The repugnance of the most adventurous states to the extrava-
gant pretensions of Spain and Portugal was quickened
and stimulated by the knowledge, that their title was
founded in the main on a partition of the eastern and
western oceans by an authority which the new
maritime nations, the Dutch and the English, no
longer reverenced—the Pope.   Thus the widely
prevailing exclusive maritime Sovereignty of early
days declined.   The English claims dwindled to

claims over territorial water close to the coast, and over portions of the sea interposed between promontory and promontory known as the King's Chambers, and over the whole of the narrow seas for ceremonial purposes ; these last claims were once so serious that even Philip II. of Spain was fired into by an English captain for flying his flag when he came into the narrow seas for the purpose of marrying our Queen Mary.

The language of the ordinance of Hastings, attributed to King John, was even much stronger :

'If a lieutenant of the King do encounter upon the sea any ships or vessels, laden or unladen, that will not strike or veil their bonets at the commandment of the lieutenant of the King, he will fight against them of the fleet ; if they be taken they be reported as enemies, and their ships and goods taken and forfeited as the goods of enemies.'

I have already spoken of the doubts entertained by English judges, and expressed in the 'Franconia' case, as to that jurisdiction over three miles or a league which is said to exist over territorial waters. If those opinions be examined, it will seem that the doubts chiefly rest on the fluctuations and differences of view as to the exact extent of territorial water which may be claimed under the general rule of International Law. In some cases the claim is identical with that of the international writers to Sovereignty for three

miles over the water next adjoining the shores. In
other cases the claim is larger. It is easy to understand these differences if we bring home to our minds
that what took place was a renunciation of indefinite
for definite claims, entailing generally a contraction
of the extent of sea asserted to be within a given
jurisdiction.

Another survival of larger pretensions is the
English claim to exclusive authority over what were
called the King's Chambers. These are portions of
the sea cut off by lines drawn from one promontory
of our coasts to another, as from the Land's End
to Milford Haven. The claim has been followed in
America, and a jurisdiction of the like kind is asserted
by the United States over Delaware Bay and other
estuaries which enter into portions of their territory.
A more indefinite claim was advanced by British
sovereigns to a larger extent of the water by the
prohibition which they issued against the roving or,
as the technical word was, the hovering of foreign
ships of war near the neutral coasts and harbours
of Great Britain. In more recent times what was
known as the 'Hovering Act' was passed, in 1736,
and this assumes for certain revenue purposes a jurisdiction of four leagues from the coast by prohibiting
foreign goods to be transhipped within that distance
without payment of duties. The United States here
again have copied this provision, and in either

country the statutory legislation has been declared
by the courts of justice to be consistent with the law
and usage of nations. The once extensive but now
greatly diminished claims of Great Britain have not
been exclusively of advantage to her. We have a
trace of the amplitude of the old claim in the
necessity which Great Britain has submitted to of
great expenditure on the costly duty of lighting by
lighthouses and in other ways a much larger extent
of seaway than is clearly under her jurisdiction.

The jurisdiction of a state over a portion of the
sea nearest its coasts, either as a fragment of ancient
claims or under the rule of International Law, is
often said to exist by virtue of a fiction under which
water is treated as land. You will find on examining
the opinions of the judges in the 'Franconia' case that
the admissibility or otherwise of such a fiction fills
considerable space in the arguments. Conversely, the
full Sovereignty of a state over the portions of land
which it includes, and which are covered by water,
rivers and lakes, might be supposed to exist under the
Law of Nature. But this apparent natural complete-
ness of Sovereignty is limited, as is seen in one case
which has had more than its share of attention from
international writers. Wherever, as often happens
in a river of great length, it passes through the
territory of a considerable number of states, it has
been asserted that each one of those states has a right

G

of navigation to the sea; and it has even been claimed
that wholly foreign states can navigate the river
from its mouth up to any one of the co-riparian
sovereignties. It is the fact that such a right as
I have described has been exercised in all great
European rivers for many centuries, and I believe
the reason to be one which every traveller along such
a river as the Rhine will at once understand. The
command of a portion of the river was not valued in
former days for the purpose of obstructing or closing
it : its advantage consisted in the tolls which were
exacted from a vessel as it passed from one sovereignty to another, and the long rivers were burdened
with obligatory payments of this kind down to the
mouth. Of course the burden was excessively heavy
on the Rhine owing to the number of semi-sove-
reignties or fractional sovereignties which abounded
within the limits of the Empire. In one instance a
portion of the Rhine was absolutely closed under a
provision of the Treaty of Westphalia. The Scheldt,
or passage through the Dutch territory at the mouth,
was closed to every other co-riparian Power, and was
free only to the Dutch themselves. There was some
pretext for this exceptional rule, because no doubt
this portion of the Rhine was mainly the work of
Dutch industry, for the river enters there into the
gigantic constructions which have been made by
Dutch engineers and by Dutch labourers for the

purpose of protecting or recovering the Dutch territory from the sea. The closing of the Scheldt was, however, never in favour with the international writers, and was for a great length of time strongly objected to. It has a gloomy celebrity, for it was the forcible opening of this passage by the French in favour of the Flemings and against the Dutch which led to the entrance of our own country into the war of the French Revolution.

Some writers on International Law have asserted that the innocent navigation, as the phrase runs, of a river circumstanced like the Rhine, existed by nature. This was controverted by the others, and the question is one of the great topics of argument in International Law. The discussion, as sometimes happens, has been much embarrassed by the use of terms of dubious meaning. Those who denied the right generally, allowed that there was an imperfect right to the privilege claimed. These terms ' perfect' and ' imperfect right' descend to us from the Roman Law, where an imperfect law is a law without a sanction. John Austin has examined these terms 'imperfect' and ' perfect law,' and asserts that in such cases the lawgiver, though he has indicated his intention, has forgotten or accidentally omitted to impose penalties on disobedience. Such a use of words is altogether out of place in International Law, because in that system there is never any direct sanction,

since there is no common sovereign. Consequently
'imperfect law' and 'imperfect right' have gradually
attained a different sense in later International Law.
Sometimes the words were used to imply that it
would be fair and reasonable to concede the liberty
claimed, sometimes it seems to have meant that a
state alleged to lie under an imperfect obligation may
concede the privilege, but might consult its own
convenience as to the method of concession. If this
way of expressing the conflicting doctrines had
always been followed, it is a not inconvenient basis
for practically settling the question. Many states
will acknowledge an imperfect duty which would refuse to allow a perfect right in any sense of the
words.

On this basis, however, that of imperfect right,
the passage of rivers has been largely regulated
by treaty. The Rhine and the Elbe were placed
under special regulations in 1814 and 1815, after
the close of the great war, by which all the states
along their banks had a right of access to the
sea. In 1828 there began a violent dispute between
England and the United States as to the power of
navigating the St. Lawrence. The St. Lawrence is
in point of fact the outlet by which the water of the
great lakes or fresh-water inland seas escapes from
the continent of America into the Atlantic. England
claimed, as owner of the territory near the mouth, to

close the St. Lawrence at pleasure, though she never
exercised the power which she assumed. On the
other hand, the United States, as sovereign owners
of valuable territory abutting on some of the great
lakes, assumed a free right of navigation to the mouth
of the St. Lawrence. Both Powers claimed more
than they hoped to obtain. The language of the
English Foreign Office assumed that England had
a perfect right to forbid the navigation of the river.
The United States seemed to assert that the whole
river was open to themselves, and perhaps to navigators of all civilised states. The controversy ended
in 1854 much in the same way as the disputes about
passage down the Rhine, and the principles here
applied were shortly afterwards applied to the great
rivers of South America. They were all thrown
open, the Parana, the Uruguay, and the Amazons.
This liberality perhaps was more due to an increased
perception of the advantages of commerce than to
the adoption of either one or other of the alleged
rules of International Law. In all cases, however,
the legal view of the matter is that the riparian
states have assented to an arrangement based on an
imperfect right.

I have spoken at the close of my last lecture of the intricate controversies in International
Law which have a fiction for a base. Perhaps
the fiction most celebrated among international

lawyers is that of ex-territoriality. The fiction of
ex-territorality is in fact founded on a metaphor.
A man in a foreign country or a ship in foreign waters
is conceived as still within the limits of the original
sovereignty to which he belonged. Sometimes, it
has been said, the ship is conceived as a portion
of the sovereign state floating about in the high sea
or elsewhere. The word seems to have been originally used to describe the privileges of ambassadors
in foreign states, and it describes them as vividly
and on the whole as accurately as a metaphor can.
The main drawback to the use of such metaphors in
legal discussion is that men, and particularly lawyers,
begin in time to conceive the metaphor as having an
existence of its own, and they make it the starting
point for new inferences which themselves are often
metaphorical.

This peculiarity remarkably distinguished another
employment of the figure of which I am speaking. The jurists of some nations contend that
the ships of a state are ex-territorial when in the
territorial waters of another state. This is again
denied by others, and various very difficult questions have arisen in quite recent times through the
ambiguity of the terms employed. We may take as
an example of this the controversy which arose fourteen or fifteen years ago as to the duty of captains of
ships of war in regard to fugitive slaves. Ships of

the British Government were constantly lying in the territorial water of independent states in the Eastern seas ; for example, in the Persian Gulf within the territorial water of Persia or within the territorial water of Turkey.   If a Man-of-War lying in its territorial water was under the jurisdiction of the state to which the neighbouring coast belonged, one treatment of a very difficult case was incumbent on her captain which would become wholly different if a ship-of-war remained within the territorial water of the state whose flag it was flying.   This case was that of the fugitive slave escaping to a British Man-of-War.   It frequently arose, for it was generally known among the populations near the coast that the English laws did not allow or pay any regard to the status of slavery.   If the ship was within the law of the neighbouring territory, there could be no question that the fugitive should be given up again to his master.   On the other hand, if the ship were subject to the law of the country whose flag it sailed under, then it became the duty of the captain to carry away the fugitive and to put him on shore in some place where he would not be again reduced to slavery.   Conflicting reports reached this country as to what was the practice in these seas, and a large commission, consisting chiefly of lawyers, was appointed for the purpose of determining the practice and deciding what the law ought to be.   The discussions which followed may be compared with those in the ' Franconia ' case for the number of topics of International Law which they included. In the long run the commission came to an agreement. Some of them thought that a British ship in Turkish water was for all purposes ex-territorial and under British Sovereignty. Others thought that it was for the time under the Sovereignty of the Turkish Government. But it was unanimously determined by the commissioners that, whichever view prevailed, a British officer could not lawfully be called upon to give up a fugitive in any case where the result of surrendering him would be to expose him to ill usage.

What I have said applies to Men-of-War, to public ships flying the flag of their own sovereign, but the fiction of ex-territoriality has had a wider scope than when applied to such ships. All through the great war at the beginning of the century the United States maintained that even private vessels ought to be considered as ex-territorial and as retaining the law of the country to which their owners belonged. This pretension was stoutly combated by Great Britain. The controversy really turned on one peculiar practice of the British Navy in those days. Being manned by impressment in its own country, its captains sought to supply insufficiency in their crews by examining the ships of neutral nations which they met, and taking out of them any sailors who were found to be of British nationality. They argued (and that this is the rule we shall see hereafter) that every private neutral ship on the high sea is liable to be searched in order that a belligerent vessel may be satisfied that there are no goods belonging to an enemy on board. For this purpose a British captain had the right of entering a friendly neutral ship ; and being there lawfully, it was argued by the British lawyers and Courts that he could take away and remove to his own ship sailors engaged in the navigation of the neutral ship who were subjects of Great Britain. No dispute was ever more violent than this, and it led directly to the war between the United States and Great Britain which began in 1814. It is happily not probable that any such dispute will occur again, although there is no absolute impediment to its revival in the decisions of Courts or in law books. Impressment is now given up by the British Government, and if in some future war Great Britain is compelled to supply its ships with crews through compulsion, resort will almost certainly be had to some other expedient. It is not impossible that we may have to copy the system which is in force in France and Germany, of a conscription confined to the maritime population. It should also be borne in

mind that in the Men-of-War of our day, which are
machines of the highest elaborateness and delicacy,
worked by steam and hydraulic power, the numbers
of the crew relatively to the size of the vessel are much
smaller than they were in the early maritime wars of
the century, so that the probability of the ship being
placed in real difficulty from the insufficiency of her
crew is considerably diminished.

The extreme form of the fiction of ex-territoriality
which the Americans put forward in respect of private
ships is thus not likely to be advanced again, because
the provocation which elicited it is very unlikely to
recur ; and indeed if an American proposal on which
I shall have to say much hereafter, that all private
property on the sea shall be exempt from capture, were
to be adopted by the general agreement of nations,
the ex-territoriality of merchant ships might possibly
be expunged from International Law by international
agreement, because the rights of visiting and searching
neutral merchant ships in time of war would disappear
of themselves. But it must be understood that at
present this claim to ex-territoriality has never been
formally negatived or set aside. The treaty between
Great Britain and the United States which closed the
war of 1814 says nothing on this subject or on the subject of the grievances which were the foundation of the
claim, and I suppose that an American lawyer would

be bound by the decisions of his own National Courts to assert it, at least abstractedly. What I have said, it will be seen, applies solely to private vessels. With regard to public vessels, Men-of-War, there is a much nearer approach to uniformity of practice and doctrine. On the whole, the position that a public ship flying the flag of the sovereign of an independent country is under the law of that country, even when in the territorial waters of another country, is accepted by the Courts and lawyers of the civilised world. But a distinction is drawn between acts of which the consequences begin and end on board the ship and take no effect externally to her, and acts done on board which have an external operation. In the first case the jurisdiction of the sovereign to whom the ship belongs is exclusive. In the second, the sovereign in whose waters the ship is lying may demand redress for the illegality, but it must be demanded from the Government which is sovereign owner of the vessel. The cases may be illustrated by occurrences which have actually happened. One sailor on board a Man-of-War lying in territorial water shoots another ; or a sailor fires a rifle from the deck of the ship and kills a native of the neighbouring country. In the first case, the captain may deal at once with the offender as the law and usage of his own country permit. In the second, he must wait until a demand is made upon his sovereign. I have already mentioned the exceptional case of a fugitive slave taking refuge on board a foreign public ship in territorial water. The decision of the commissioners did not settle any principle, but established a working rule which is sufficient for the occasion.

LECTURE V.

NAVAL OR MARITIME BELLIGERENCY.

To sum up what I have been saying. I have been discussing certain legal fictions which are signified through legal metaphors, and especially one of them by which places and things not actually within the territorial jurisdiction of a state are supposed to be within that state for the purpose of collecting into a group the rules of law which apply to them. This fiction of ex-territoriality, is applied by general consent to the residences and persons of ambassadors and diplomatic agents in foreign countries, and on the whole the law on these subjects is expressed with sufficient accuracy by the fiction before us. By most nations the fiction is also applied to the portions of sea adjacent to the coast and deemed to be what is called the territorial waters of a particular state ; that is to say, water which, so far as water can be assimilated to land, is regarded as part of the state's territory. Finally, by some communities a merchant ship on the high sea is alleged to be ex-territorial—to be in the

same position as the territory of the country to which
she belongs. In this last way the fiction before us
has become mixed with a very important branch of
law, the law of Naval Belligerency, and I use it as a
convenient point of transit to that subject which I
might take up at several places in these lectures, but
which I wish to include in this portion of them for
several cogent reasons. It is a province of law which
rose into extreme importance at the end of the last century and the beginning of the present ; it has long
been, and still is, the field of many bitter disputes ;
it is a part of International Law in which a great reform
has recently been attempted ; and though the attempt
partially miscarried, the cause of failure deserves our
attention on a variety of grounds ; it sheds light on
certain weaknesses of the international system, and
raises a very serious question as to the true interests
of England in a reform of that system which all but
obtained the assent of the civilised world.

I proceed, therefore, to deal with naval or maritime belligerency in its effects on belligerent Powers
and on neutrals. The elements of the subject are
simple. When two states go to war, the ships, public
and private, of one are, relatively to the other, so many
articles of movable property floating on the sea.
The capture of one of them by a ship of the other
belligerent is *primâ facie* regulated by the same principle as the seizure on land of a valuable movable by a

soldier or body of soldiers. The law on the subject descends to us directly from the Roman Law. The property of an enemy is one of those things which the Roman Law in one of its oldest portions considers to be *res nullius*—no man's property. It may be taken just as a wild bird or wild animal is taken, by seizing it with the intention to keep it ; but it is expressly laid down that a wild animal if it escapes ceases to be the property of the captor ; and the question is, when is the captured property so reduced to possession as to make it altogether the property of the captor ?

There was much dispute on this point among the interpreters of Roman Law. Some, including Grotius, maintained that the proper test was time, and the thing had to be possessed by the captor for four-and-twenty hours. A trace of this rule may be seen in the alleged power of the maritime captor to destroy the vessel which he has taken when he has no means of bringing it into a port. There is, however, another rule of Roman origin which has gradually supplanted the first mentioned. The captor must take the captured property *infra præsidia*, within the fortified lines of a Roman camp. This applied to maritime warfare means nowadays at sea a port of the captor's country, as distinguished from an open roadstead, or the port of an ally of the captor or the port of a neutral Power. As it is sometimes put, the ship must be taken into military possession ; that is, into a possession from

which it cannot be rescued otherwise than by force.
But in order that the captor may have the full benefit
of his capture, yet another condition must be satisfied.
The captured ship and its cargo, or cargo belonging to
the enemy but found in a neutral ship, must be taken
before a prize court and condemned as lawful prize.
Till this condemnation has taken place the purchaser
of the captured property could not be sure that he had
a complete title to it, and could not obtain full value
for it if he sold it.

Prize courts are sometimes called international
courts, and no doubt modern International Law does,
to some extent, recognise them ; but in principle a
prize court is a court established by positive municipal law, and it is entrusted by the sovereign of the
state in which it is established with the duty of
deciding whether ship or cargo is prize or no prize.
In the abstract its object is to satisfy the conscience
of the sovereign that the captures made by his subjects are valid captures. He is always, in theory,
supposed to be responsible for them. But the great
practical function of a prize court is to decide between the belligerent sovereign's subjects and subjects of neutral states. Neutral goods may form part
of the cargo found in the enemy's ship which has
been legally captured ; or, again, cargo belonging to
the other belligerent may have been found on the
high sea in a neutral ship ; or, again, the vessel brought
into port may have been unlawfully captured through

having been in the territorial waters of a neutral state, or by an attack organised in such territorial waters.   In both of these cases capture is forbidden. If the belligerent sovereign permitted them, he would be guilty of an injury to an unoffending neutral.

The capture of ship or cargo belonging to one belligerent by the armed ships of the other is part of the fortune of war ; nor can the captor much complain of having to bring his prize into a port for condemnation. So far as the captured vessel is concerned, this hardship is somewhat mitigated by the practice of what is called 'ransoming.'   The commander willing to pro-. mise a definite sum for ship or cargo prepares a document which is called a ' Ransom Bill.'   It is drawn in duplicate.   The capturing officer takes one copy, and the commander of the captured ship another ; and this ransom bill operates as a safe-conduct to the captured vessel on her voyage to a separate port.   So far as relates to cruisers of the other belligerent, she enjoys immunity from their power of capturing her unless she has varied her course so as to raise suspicion of an intention to escape.

The real hardships of capture at sea, to which a large part of the world is not, even now, reconciled, are those affecting neutrals.   If an enemy's ship at sea contains neutral cargo, the neutral must submit to have his goods taken into port for adjudication, and must of course forego opportunities of obtaining a

H

favourable market, though his goods are not liable
to capture. If a neutral ship contains admittedly
enemy's cargo, the captain must submit to have
his goods transhipped. These rules are of much
antiquity. They are found in one of those treatises
which are authorities on International Law, but
which are older than its recognised beginning. In
the 'Consolato del Mare,' which is supposed to contain
the maritime usages of the seas which formed part of
the Mediterranean basin, there are various laws with
reference to the capture of neutral ships and neutral
cargo, and enemy's cargo in neutral bottoms. These
seas were, in the days in which these usages grew up,
full of small commercial ports, all manufacturing and
exporting, and not situated at great distances from
one another. The origin of the rule which we are
discussing exactly fits in with the relations of a
certain number of small sovereignties of this kind ;
and that this is really the origin of the rule before us
is indicated by provisions relating to the interruption
of voyage, as for example by rules compelling the
neutral ship to change her course for the port of the
captor, and providing that she shall have compensation
for her loss of time. The condition of these seas
which I have sketched—a number of small towns
engaged in actual commerce, but not separated from
one another by any great length of sea—goes far to
explain this ancient maritime law ; but as one mari-

time Power and another grew in strength and came to
value the advantages of neutrality, the discontent with
these old rules began, and a desire arose for a more
general and simpler system.   One, in fact, which grew
up was looked upon with much favour.   It is often
denoted by a sort of jingle which does not convey a
real antithesis : ' Enemy ships, enemy goods ; free
ships, free goods.'   All the cargo found in a hostile
vessel may be made prize ; if the vessel itself belong
to a neutral, all the goods shall be treated as neutral
property and shall not be liable to capture.   France
was on one side with a severe rule confiscating the
neutral ship when any hostile cargo was carried in it,
while the Dutch were for a system more lenient to
neutrals, and finally France herself became patroness
of this rule.

Many treaties have been negotiated between
civilised states which embodied either both these rules
or one of them ; but still the rule which enables the
belligerent to capture hostile cargo wherever he finds
it, was on the whole that which lay at the base of
International Law.   The first serious attempt to effect
a general reform of this principle was undertaken at
the close of the Crimean war ; and in 1854 the
Powers which had taken part in, or had been most
directly interested in, that war, issued what was called
the Declaration of Paris.   After reciting that maritime law in time of war had been the subject of

deplorable disputes ; that the uncertainty of this law gave rise to differences of opinion which might occasion serious differences and even conflicts, the plenipotentiaries at Paris, seeking to introduce into international relations fixed principles on the subject before them, declare that they have adopted the following summary of the rules which they wish to see carried into practice : First, privateering is abolished ; second, the neutral flag covers enemy's goods with the exception of contraband of war ; third, neutral goods, with the exception of contraband of war, are not liable to capture under the enemy's flag ; fourth, blockades in order to be binding must be effective ; that is to say, maintained by a force sufficient really to prevent access to the coast of the enemy. The net result shows that the rule, free ships make free goods, was adopted ; but the other rule which has so often been coupled with it, enemy ships make enemy goods, was not adopted.

This Declaration was adhered to by all the Powers who had joined in the Crimean war, and it seemed for awhile that it would receive the assent of the whole of the civilised world, thus forming the first great example of a reform of the Law of Nations resting on the basis of expressly pledged faith instead of the older foundation of precedent and ancient rule. But ôn the Declaration being submitted to the United States, the Government of that country objected to the first article, 'Privateering is abolished.' A privateer is an armed private ship commissioned by a belligerent sovereign to depredate on the commerce of his enemy, and rewarded by a share of the capture, which in recent times has amounted nearly to the whole of it. The reason given for the refusal of the United States by Mr. Marcy, the Secretary of State, was plausible enough :

' The United States consider powerful navies and large standing armies as permanent establishments to be detrimental to national prosperity and dangerous to civil liberty. The expense of keeping them up is burdensome to the people ; they are in some degree a menace to peace among nations. A large force ever ready to be devoted to the purposes of war is a temptation to rush into it. The policy of the United States has ever been, and never more than now, adverse to such establishments, and they can never be brought to acquiesce in any change in International Law which may render it necessary for them to maintain a powerful navy or large standing army in time of peace. If forced to vindicate their rights by arms, they are content, in the present aspect of international relations, to rely in military operations on land mainly upon volunteer troops, and for the protection of their commerce in no inconsiderable degree upon their mercantile marine. If this country were deprived of these resources it would be obliged to change

its policy and assume a military attitude before the
world.   In resisting an attempt to change the existing maritime law that may produce such a result, it
looks beyond its own interest, and embraces in its
view the interest of such nations as are not likely to be
dominant naval Powers.   Their situation in this respect is similar to that of the United States, and to
them the protection of commerce and the maintenance
of international relations of peace appeal as strongly
as to this country to withstand the proposed change
in the settled Law of Nations.   To such nations the
surrender of the right to resort to privateers would
be attended with consequences most adverse to their
commercial prosperity without any compensating
advantages. . . .

'It certainly ought not to excite the least surprise that strong naval Powers should be willing to
forego the practice, comparatively useless to them, of
employing privateers, upon condition that weaker
Powers agree to part with their most effective means
of defending their maritime rights.   It is in the
opinion of this Government to be seriously appre-
hended that if the use of privateers be abandoned, the
dominion over the seas will be surrendered to those
Powers which adopt the policy and have the means
of keeping up large navies.   The one which has a
decided naval superiority would be potentially the
mistress of the ocean, and by the abolition of priva-

teering that domination would be more firmly secured. Such a Power engaged in a war with a nation inferior in naval strength would have nothing to do for the security and protection of its commerce but to look after the ships of the regular navy of its enemy. These might be held in check by one-half or less of its naval force, and the other might sweep the commerce of its enemy from the ocean. Nor would the injurious effect of a vast naval superiority to weaker states be much diminished if that superiority were shared among three or four great Powers. It is unquestionably the interest of such weaker states to discountenance and resist a measure which fosters the growth of regular naval establishments.'

It is at the same time to be remarked that this opinion, though intelligible, had not always prevailed, and that early in their history the United States had negotiated, through Benjamin Franklin, a treaty with Prussia in 1785 by which it was stipulated that in the event of war neither Power should commission privateers. On the other hand, an early president of the American Union, Monroe, had laid down that it was unworthy of civilised states to prey upon private property when in transit at sea. The result of the refusal of the United States to assent to the Declaration of 1854 was that this Declaration has not become part of the general law of other civilisations, for the assent of a state which is perhaps

destined to be the most powerful in the world, and
certainly the most powerful neutral state in the world,
has been withheld from it.   But the United States
Government expressed its willingness to join in a
modified form of the Declaration, if all private property at sea should be exempted from capture, as
President Monroe had argued that it ought to be ; and
there is good reason to believe that if the signataries
of the Declaration would agree to this exemption of
private property, the United States would withdraw
their objection to the abolition of privateering.

The first article of the Declaration was invoked
in a dispute which arose between the French and
Prussian Governments, then at war, during the contest of 1870.   The Prussian Government, soon to be
merged in that of Germany, proposed to raise a volunteer navy.   All German seafaring men were to offer
themselves for service in a Federal navy for the whole
period of the then proceeding war.   The French
Government objected to this as a breach of the first
article of the Declaration.   They declared that it was
a species of revival of privateering.   Some writers,
including Mons. Calvo, and to a certain extent Mr.
Hall, have supported these views ; but some conditions
of the service proposed to be established, as for
example the necessity for the volunteers wearing a
uniform, the incorporation of the new force with the
existing navy, and an oath to articles of war, seem to

me to take these naval volunteers out of the class of
privateers. As a matter of fact, the Decree was never
practically acted upon.

It will be seen from the text of the Declaration
of Paris, which is set forth above, that its rules
do not apply in two cases : first, where contraband of war is carried in a ship ; and next, in the
case of a ship endeavouring to obtain entrance to a
blockaded town.   Therefore the law of contraband of
war and the law of blockade are not touched by the
reform under the Declaration of Paris, except so far as
a principle long contended for is applied to blockades.

From the very beginning of International Law a
belligerent has been allowed to prevent a neutral from
supplying his enemy with things capable of being
used immediately in war. Such things are called
technically 'Contraband of War,' and may be condemned independently of all question as to the neutrality of the owner. The ship and cargo are taken
into a port of the captor ; the contraband is condemned in a prize court, but the fate of the ship
itself varies. If the ship belongs to the owner of the
contraband, or if the owner of the ship is privy to the
carriage of the contraband, the ship is condemned ;
but not so if the ship belongs to a different owner,
who knows nothing of the destination of the contraband commodities. This branch of International
Law is complex and difficult, but it owes its intricacy

and difficulty to one special question : what are the
articles stigmatised as contraband ? From the very
first, Grotius had laid down that things directly used
in war—for example, weapons—were contraband. He
also ruled that things useless in war, articles of luxury
as he described them, were not contraband. But outside these categories there were a great number of
things capable of employment both in war and peace
—*res ancipitis usus*—and it is in regard to these that
innumerable questions have arisen. Are articles of
naval construction—for example, the raw materials of
sails and cordage—contraband ? Do they become so
at any particular stage of manufacture ? Are iron,
brass, steel, &c. contraband ? Are coals and horses?
Are provisions contraband ? To these questions all
sorts of answers have been given. In many special
treaties the list of contraband and non-contraband
commodities is given, and the practice of states is
extremely various. On the whole the most general
rule which can be laid down is that, with the exception of weapons or munitions of war, the contraband,
or non-contraband, character of the cargo must
depend on its destination, and on the nature of the
particular war which is going on. The commodity
most recently sought to be brought into the list as
contraband is coal. England, the great exporter of
coal, refused to admit its being necessarily contraband ; but in the war of 1870 the English Government declined to allow British coal to be carried to a

French fleet that was lying in the North Sea. The most vehement of the disputes has been, perhaps, that about provisions. At the end of the last century, when the great war of the Revolution had begun, English statesmen believed the French population to be on the point of starvation ; and that the French were suffering great distress from scarcity of food is now most fully established. The English Government therefore seized all ships bound to a French port which were laden with provisions. As their enemy was believed by them to be on the point of abandoning the contest through want of provisions, they refused to allow the stock of provisions to be increased. Just at the same moment the United States had become the great neutral Power enjoying the advantages of the carrying trade, and the Government of the United States issued a series of vehement protests against the assumption of the contraband character of provisions in any circumstances. It is probable that in future provisions will only be contraband when destined for a port in which an enemy's fleet is lying. The point on which I desire to fix your attention is that the test of articles which are contraband of war is not yet settled.

The other portion of the older law which is not affected by the Declaration of Paris is Blockade. Blockade is defined as the interruption by a belligerent of access to a place, or to territory, which is in possession of an enemy. Blockade is probably confined to maritime

hostilities; but it has considerable external resemblance
to a siege by land, and the law of the one acting by land
has visibly affected the law of the other acting by sea.
But as a matter of fact the objects of blockade and
siege are not the same. The aim of a siege is the
capture of a strong place or town beset. The aim of
a blockade is to put stress on the population of a
port, or on the population behind it, through denying
it communication, commercial or otherwise, with the
rest of the world accessible to it only by sea. This
it effects by the rules of International Law, which
permit blockading ships to capture ships of the other
belligerent which attempt to enter the blockaded
port, or to come out of it, or which may reasonably
be suspected of having this intention.

There are two main conditions of the capture of
neutral vessels by a blockading squadron. One is
that they must be warned of the existence of the
blockade. The mode of giving this notice required
by law varies in different countries. France and
certain other countries give notice to each ship indi-
vidually, their cruisers stopping it, and seeing that
the stoppage is notified on the ship's papers. England
and the United States make public notice in their
own territory, and communicate the fact of the
blockade to foreign Powers. Under modern circumstances, where information is conveyed over the
civilised world by newspapers and the electric tele-

graph, it certainly seems that the English and American practice is sufficient. It is hardly possible that there should be ignorance nowadays of the existence of an established blockade.

The second condition is that mentioned in the Declaration of Paris : the blockade must be effective; that is, it must be maintained by a naval force strong enough to prevent access to the blockaded coast. It is the act of secretly evading a force on the whole adequate which constitutes the offence that subjects a neutral ship to capture—what is called 'running the blockade.' The stress laid on the sufficiency of the blockade is a legacy from the last century. Hardly any country has not been at some time or other accused of establishing what is called a 'paper blockade;' that is to say, publicly announcing the blockade of a particular portion of the coast, but not supporting it by a sufficient force of ships. It is justly thought that such a blockade gives the maximum of annoyance to honest neutrals, but allows a maximum number of dishonest neutral adventurers to penetrate the line. Nothing can justify the absolute interdiction of a portion of the coast to neutral commerce except a method likely on the whole to secure that end. A blockade must as a general rule be continuously maintained, but an exception is allowed in the case of ships driven away by storm and stress of weather.

LECTURE VI.

THE DECLARATION OF PARIS.

ONE point of considerable interest in International Law is the very different degree of durability which the various parts of the system have proved to possess. The oldest rules which belong to its structure are simply rules of religion and morality ordinarily applied between man and man, but so modified by the international writers as to be capable of application between state and state. By the side of these are some rules which have been inherited from the oldest stratum of the Roman Law, rules of great simplicity, and distinguished at the same time by a great amount of common sense. These rules still survive and are still available for the solution of international questions. On the other hand, there are parts of International Law which are comparatively modern, which are highly complex, and which in their day were of great importance, but which have now become thoroughly obsolete through changes in the social condition of nations or international intercourse. A good example may be

pointed out in what was once known as the Rule of
the War of 1756. If you look into an international
discussion dating from the latter part of the last century, if you look into the reports of the decisions of
courts belonging to the same epoch, you will find
constant allusions to this rule, which ultimately became
the subject of a serious quarrel between England and
the United States, a sovereign community which had
not been in existence when the rule was first heard
of. England, like probably all the nations of the
European continent, adhered to the doctrine that
trade with colonies and dependencies was the exclusive privilege of the subjects of the mother country.
The question arose whether war made any difference
to this monopoly. When the mother country became
a belligerent, the route followed by the colonial trade
was less obstructed than in ordinary times. The
ships which watched the foreigner who in peace tried
to intrude upon it, were perhaps driven away by the
vessels of the other belligerent ; and the route being
more open, neutrals constantly tried to engage in
trade which in time of peace would have been forbidden to them. What, then, was the consequence of
neutral invasions of this privilege? It was argued
on behalf of the neutral trader, that there being nobody
else to undertake the transport of commodities, he
was entitled to share in it. This was denied by the
English courts of justice, and they decided that a

neutral ship, engaged in a trade of this description, was liable to capture. This was the rule of the war of 1756, which denied to neutral shipowners participation in the trade which was a monopoly of the mother country or the country which was sovereign over the dependency. There was at that time a rule which forbade certain articles to be exported from Ireland ; and of course the trade of India, which was in the hands of a company, was even less open to non-privileged traders. But this rule, and the state of things which it implied, are now completely obsolete, and all the dissertations about them which once filled the books are obsolete. It was the United States, then new as a sovereign community, which first contested most strongly the legality of the rule. But it has been in fact destroyed by the indirect influence of the United States. The fortune of the United States showed that a great increase of national wealth followed independence, and the demonstrable profitableness of open trade sapped the old colonial theories, while, no doubt, the success of the United States in securing their independence showed the danger of attempting to control extensive and distant dependencies.

A specially interesting set of questions arises on the four articles of the Declaration of Paris, the great modern system of reformed maritime law which, but for one dissentient, would have become the law of the

whole civilised world. This Declaration, as we have
seen, keeps alive two sub-departments of the old law
of nations in very much their original state ; the law
of contraband of war, and the law of blockade. Let
us ask ourselves whether these branches of law are
likely to be long-lived even as slightly altered by the
arrangements of Paris. I have already pointed out
that the list of articles of contraband of war was not
yet closed. The proposal to include certain things
in this class has not in some cases been conclusively
rejected, while, on the other hand, as it is very
generally allowed that commodities may become
contraband through the circumstances of a particular
war, perfectly new kinds of contraband may yet make
their appearance. Perhaps the articles as to which
there has been most dispute have been those which
follow the first class and head the second ; the first
class being munitions of war, and the second class
things of what, in International Law, are called
' doubtful use ; ' timber, sail cloth, hemp in the early
stages of manufacture, cordage, pitch and tar. Lord
Stowell admits this, and gives the reason, that wars
have become more and more naval, so that articles of
most use in regard to ships, and the propulsion of
ships, gain more and more likeness to munitions of
war. There were endless controversies on the subject. There were repeated differences with the Baltic
Powers in whose territories the materials of these

things were for the most part produced. Many
treaties gave lists of articles of contraband, and to
some of these England was a party. The principle
which the English Government several times adopted
was, that naval stores might be taken possession of,
but that, unlike articles of contraband, they must be
paid for by the captor. But changes in the structure
and mode of propulsion of ships tend to make this
kind of contraband or quasi-contraband obsolete.
Steam renders sails of little utility, and diminishes
their number. The hulls are now more and more
made of iron, and iron wire even takes the place of
cordage. It is possible that naval stores may disappear from the list of contraband, while there may
be a struggle to include such innocent articles as coal
and food.

The second exception to the immunity of neutral
property is, property carried in a ship attempting,
or reasonably suspected of attempting, to enter a
blockaded port. Blockades in the last century were
considered by belligerents a most effective method
of distressing an enemy ; and over great part of the
European continent the great markets for traders
and the fortified stations for ships are most exposed
to blockade. To prevent neutral vessels from entering or leaving these ports, was to do severe injury to
trade ; and to impoverish the blockaded port was to
impoverish the country round about, and, if ships of

war were lying within the port, to diminish seriously
the total fighting force of the enemy. Brest and
Toulon were practically blockaded all through the great
war at the beginning of this century and the end of
the last. England was again a belligerent during the
Crimean war, and there were some blockades, not
perhaps very important, of ports in the Baltic and
the Black Sea. But during the American war between the Northern and Southern States she became
a neutral, it having been at last allowed, even by the
United States, that there was a state of belligerency
between the combatants. Even then it became clear
that a considerable change had occurred. Steam
made the limited navy of the Northern States able to
maintain a fairly effective blockade of nearly the
whole coast of the Southern Confederate States.
Steam also greatly facilitated the operations of the
neutral blockade-runners. But the land behind the
ports of the Southern States was rich and fertile, and
many railways had been constructed in those territories. The effect, therefore, of the blockade was very
unlike the effect of the blockades in the great French
war. Articles of first necessity were easily supplied
to the blockaded ports from within, and the effect of
the blockade was to raise the price of luxuries, which
were always imported from abroad. If, however, we
look on the present state of the world, we shall see

that no European continental Power of any importance exists which is not connected by railways with the interior of the country to which it belongs, and also, through connecting links, with the railway system of the whole Continent. A blockade may still raise the price of necessaries and conveniences, but unless aided by a land siege it cannot prevent a sufficient and even plentiful supply of necessaries and conveniences entering a blockaded place. It cannot arrest trade; it can only divert it. A land traffic would at once take the place of a maritime traffic. Hardly any colonial produce reached the blockaded ports during the great war with France. Now it would flow in from a dozen openings in Eastern and North-eastern Europe. It is possible that no part of North America could now be blockaded so as to greatly distress the country behind. There has been an extensive construction of railways through all the states on the east side of the United States, and an immense multiplication of manufactures throughout the country. South America, rapidly growing in wealth but insufficiently supplied with railway communication, would be the only part of the world to which neutrals would resort, and at which blockades would be of any value.

The fact that in any future maritime war it will probably be found that these branches of law have changed their character, not through any alteration

of opinion, but through industrial development, may
suggest a suspicion that the new maritime law created
by the Declaration of Paris, though now hardly more
than thirty years old, may yet shortly prove obsolete.
The position is this. Neutral trade is relieved from
annoyance and interruption, and privateering is
abolished as regards most of the world. But the
United States decline the new neutral immunities
because they will not surrender privateering. Now
in any new war an attempt to enforce the parts of
law unfavourable to neutrals, will probably turn the
neutral trading community into a belligerent, and the
power of employing its own and foreign ships as
privateers would make the American Union a very
formidable belligerent. The question is, whether it
is worth while amending the Declaration of Paris, and
making it of universal application by accepting the
further reforms proposed by the United States ; that
is, by exempting all private property from capture, and
by abolishing privateering.

Let us first ask ourselves : what is supposed to be
the object in war of subjecting the property of an
enemy to capture, either in his own ships or in
neutral bottoms ? It does not directly benefit the
country carrying out the law, because under modern
practice a vessel properly captured belongs, not to
the State, but to the captors. The assumption is that
it distresses the enemy, that it enfeebles his trade,

and raises greatly the price of many luxuries and
commodities, and, more than all, that it seriously
diminishes his capital. It is here to be observed that
the view of maritime law taken, even by international
lawyers, does not quite answer to the truth. A
metaphor used in the last century was that the operations of maritime war resembled a flight of carrier
pigeons pursued by a flight of hawks. But he who
would repeat this figure would have to forget the
enormous growth of the practice of maritime insurance. It may happen as to war risks as with insurance against perils of the sea, that a capture of a .
man's vessel, if prudently managed, may enrich rather
than impoverish him. No doubt enhanced rates of
insurance do impoverish a nation, and do diminish its
capital. But the loss is widely diffused, it falls on
the well-to-do class, and a war must be very pro-
tracted in which increase of marine insurance would
be sensibly felt by the mass of the population.

Another general position may be noticed. In a
war in which aggression is kept on the old footing by
the powers of armament which privateering gives,
the Power which has most property at sea is most
injured. The old law took for granted the equality
not only of naval strength among states, but in
volume of trade and of property risked. To the
amount of risk the amount of loss will always corre-
spond. The question, therefore, arises : what interest

have we, what interest has Great Britain, in refusing
to grant a general immunity from capture to all private
property at sea ?   In the first place, so far as trade is
conducted by maritime conveyance, this country has
incomparably the largest share in it. This is in great
part a consequence of a revolution in shipbuilding.
So long as ships were built of wood, the maritime
Powers were those which commanded most timber.
The Baltic states, Russia, and the United States seemed
likely to have in turn a monopoly of transport.   The
Dutch swept the world for timber adapted to maritime purposes.   But now that ships of all classes are
made of iron, the monopoly of construction and possession has passed to Great Britain. We are both
the constructors and the carriers of the world, and
we suffer more than any other community from all
dangers, interruptions, and annoyances which beset
maritime carriage.

But far the most serious consideration affecting
the matter before us—that is, the conformity of the
Declaration of Paris to our permanent interests—is
the relation of maritime law, which it sets up, to the
supply of food. The statesmen of the last century,
and of the first part of this, unhesitatingly assumed
that it was the interest of this country to raise the
largest part of the food of its population from British
soil. They were used to wars, and the great French
war seemed to them to establish that a country not

fed by the produce of its own soil might be reduced
to the greatest straits. In fact, the price of corn
during the great French war, and even for some
years following it, was absolutely prodigious. This
is the secret of their protectionism, and not any
particular economical theory. They looked on the
evils of importing food from abroad as a clear de-
duction from experience. Since that period, the
infrequency of wars has kept out of sight the unexampled nature of our position with regard to food.
So far as the articles most necessary to life are concerned, we are mainly fed from other countries,
removed from us by vast distances—from North
America and from India ; that is to say, a great
part of the national food before reaching us is only
accessible to us through maritime carriage, very long
and capable of very easy interruption. Sir James
Caird, in a paper which he has recently published,
says that the food imported into Great Britain during
the year 1887 would probably reach one hundred and
forty millions sterling. Nor can the balance between
foreign commodities and home supplies be seriously
altered. Sir James Caird points out in the same
paper that Great Britain is steadily becoming a
pastoral country instead of an agricultural country.
The state of living under any circumstances is at all
times very hard to alter ; and population, at various
degrees of pace, always multiplies up to subsistence.

On the other hand, the price which we pay for our
prodigious purchase of food in other countries is
really paid by our manufactures, of which the ultimate sources are our coal and our iron, and the
inherited skill of our operative classes. Thus the
greater part of the food which we consume in any
year can only reach us through a long voyage, and
the price which is the means of bringing it to us
must also come through a voyage of equal length.
These, of course, are economical reasons, but I also
look on the subject from the point of view of International Law. Unless wars must be altogether discarded as certain never again to recur, our situation
is one of unexampled danger. Some part of the
supplies which are matter of life and death to us may
be brought to us as neutral cargo with less difficulty
than before the Declaration of Paris was issued, but
a nation still permitted to employ privateers can in-
terrupt and endanger our supplies at a great number
of points, and so can any nation with a maritime force
of which any material portion can be detached for predatory cruising. It seems, then, that the proposal of
the American Government to give up privateers on
condition of exempting all private property from
capture, might well be made by some very strong
friend of Great Britain. If universally adopted, it
would save our food, and it would save the commodities which are the price of our food, from their most

formidable enemies, and would disarm the most formidable class of those enemies.

Of course I am aware of the objections which might be made. It may be asked whether it would tend to diminish wars if economical loss were reduced to the lowest point, and if hostility between nations resolved itself into a battle of armed champions, of ironclads and trained armies, if war were to be something like the contests between the Italian States in the Middle Ages, conducted by free companies in the pay of this or that community. I think that, even thus modified, war would be greatly abated. But this is a subject which ought not to be taken for granted without discussion, and I hope in some future lecture to take it up and go into it completely.

LECTURE VII.

THE MITIGATION OF WAR.

THE age in which International Law was born was an age of land wars. The wars of succession and of feudal ascendency had partially died out, but the Reformation brought with it a new fury of fighting, and the wars of religion were among the most ferocious that mankind had waged. Armies did not then so much consist of rival potentates, as of hosts in which each individual detested every man on the other side as a misbeliever. This ferocity is generally believed to have culminated in the siege of Magdeburg. There is a famous passage of Grotius about the licence of fighting which he saw around him ; and though the dates forbid us to see here with some writers any allusion to the siege of Magdeburg, there seems little doubt that the stories of the horrors which became current gave a new point to the speculations of Grotius and his school.

Until very recent times there is great ground for distrusting the accuracy of the figures which purport to represent the amount of slaughter at battles and sieges. It is said, however, that the population of Magdeburg, which was taken by storm, was reduced from 25,000 to 2,700. The siege is described by an English eyewitness, whose account of it, generally regarded as authentic, constitutes those 'Memoirs of a Cavalier' which are generally embodied in the works of Defoe. The writer states that out of 25,000 men, and some said 30,000, there was not after the storm a soul to be seen alive till the flames drove those that were hid in vaults and secret places to seek death in the streets rather than perish in the fire. Of these miserable creatures too some were killed by the fierce soldiers, but at last they saved the lives of such as came out of their cellars and holes, and so about 2,000 poor desperate creatures were left. There was little shooting. The execution was all cutting of throats and mere house murders. Later historical information tends on the whole to relieve the memory of Count Tilly, the commander of the besiegers, from the infamy which has hitherto attached to it ; but all sieges in that day were to the last degree homicidal, and there is a general impression that the peculiar ferocity of the soldiery after the capture of a town by storm was due to the Tartars, who had twice overrun what were then the most fertile and civilised portions of the world, and who never spared the population of the town which had resisted them. They appear to have considered that every stratagem and every degree of bad faith was justifiable for the purpose of inducing the garrison to surrender, but in the long run they never spared any man.   Nor have the countries in which these massacres took place ever wholly recovered from them.   So far, indeed, as the centre and west of Europe are concerned, there is visible a calming down of these bitter extremities of war as soon as Grotius, with perhaps a few predecessors and a series of successors, began to write.   I have already several times referred to his method. He was guided, as it seems, principally by what he supposed to be examples and precedents.   He was a man of great learning according to the particular standards of learning which prevailed in that day; but the critical treatment of history had not begun, and the worst of the pile of innumerable examples which are collected in the ' De Jure Belli et Pacis ' is that we cannot be sure of the authenticity of the accounts of them which are found in the books of ancient writers.   Grotius digested these precedents.   He separated the most humane from the most ferocious, performing the function of separation by applying to the mass of matter before him, first of all the test of religious teaching as he found it in the Scriptures, and next the principle of what the Romans called the Law of Nature.   The method of his immediate successors has been substantially the same ; but in our day some scepticism has arisen, not so much as to the philosophical value of the process as with regard to its practical results.   In modern international writings you may sometimes find it said that the softening of the usages of war was not so much due to Grotius, or to writers who came after him, as to the growing humanity of military commanders.   It is true that among the successors of Grotius there is a great variety in the degree of humanity which characterises them. Puffendorf and Bynkershoek are inferior to Vattel in gentleness, and in the wish to prefer the more humane to the crueller usage, but beyond comparison the most humane of the publicists is Vattel, a Swiss. There is, however, very good reason to suppose that it was the writings of the publicists which most en-couraged the humanity of war.   They all followed Grotius in professing unbounded respect for the Roman conception of the Law of Nature.   Philosophically that principle is now not much cared for ; but the supposed rules of the Law of Nature were applied by another set of writers to another subject matter. There was a gradual growth all over continental Europe in the eighteenth century of respect and reverence, and even enthusiasm, for humanity, and you may per-ceive that on the whole the persons who expe-rienced, or pretended to experience, this feeling, were believers in the Law of Nature.   The chief of them was that famous man the whole of whose philosophy, political, social, and educational, was based on the

Law of Nature, Jean Jacques Rousseau. It seems in truth, apart from what the opinion of scholars may have been, that there was always a close association between the Law of Nature and humanity, and that by their constant profession of applying that law and of easily distinguishing its dictates from one another the international writers did materially increase the gentleness of mankind even when their passions were most excited.

The wars of the last part of the seventeenth and most of the eighteenth century were naval wars. A great amount of law grew up while they were continuing. One chief reason why, on the whole, naval usages are reasonable and humane is, that the belligerents were checked by the neutrals. In land wars a neutral can only affect proceedings to which he objects by taking part in the strife ; but from the very first the belligerent maritime Powers were prevented from going to the full lengths of predatory destructiveness by the authority of prize courts. It is, however, quite true that the commanders of land forces did gradually abandon the ferocity with which Tilly has been reproached. There was no more humane commander on the whole than our own Duke of Wellington. It is singular, at the same time, that he constantly falls into an error with which English lawyers are specially charged, that of confounding military law, which is regulating law, with martial law, which means the will of the officer commanding. He always spoke of the law of war as consisting in the volition of the Commander of the Forces.

The first great attempt which was made after the epoch of Grotius to give general fixity and to humanise the law of land war, was made almost in our day by an unfortunate sovereign to whom justice has never been fully done, Alexander II. of Russia. He does seem to have been animated, as were both the statesmen and literary men occasionally in the eighteenth century, by an enthusiasm for humanity. You are all aware that almost immediately after his succession to the Russian throne he abolished serfdom ; but his efforts to reform International Law, and specially the usages of war, are less remembered. He joined in promoting the Geneva Convention, of which I shall say much presently ; he was the author of the proposal for renouncing the use of certain weapons which caused wounds of unusual painfulness ; and he was the sovereign who summoned and who took an unflagging interest in the Brussels Convention of 1874. The Brussels Convention failed, and we shall find, I think, hereafter that the reasons why it failed are remarkably instructive. I will say that one of the grounds for its not coming to maturity was, that it was commenced too soon after one of the greatest of modern wars, which probably never had a rival in the violence of the passions which it excited. England before the Convention met had stipulated for the omission of all discussion of the rules of naval war. These, I suppose, were considered to have been sufficiently settled for the day by the Declaration of Paris ; and at the close of the discussions of the Conference, when even its members admitted that they had been able to agree on a very small part of the matters submitted to them, it was the English Foreign Secretary of State, Lord Derby, who finally gave the Convention its deathblow. Undoubtedly the smaller Powers of Europe, and the Powers which have not yet taken up the system of great armies raised by conscription, had very serious reasons for objecting to many of its suggestions, which had not unnaturally sprung up in the minds of military men who sympathised either with France or with Germany in the war which a few years before had been brought to a conclusion. The Brussels Conference had, however, one result which had great importance and interest. Just at the close of the American War of Secession the United States had prepared a Manual of Rule and Usage for the use of their officers in the field. This example—the formation of a practical Manual stating for the officers of each nation what contingencies they were to be prepared for in actual contest and how they were to deal with them—was

* K

followed by Germany, by England, and by France, and some of these Manuals have been adopted by smaller Powers. But they were all greatly affected by the recommendations of the Conference of Brussels ; and in reality it may be said that wherever there was anything like an approach to unanimity in the decisions and votes of the Conference, it is adopted in this somewhat irregular form by the greater part of the nations of the world.

The Manual prepared for English officers, which was, I believe, chiefly compiled by the present Lord Thring, then the official draftsman of the British Government, is one of the best. Visibly the writer has taken all that he could take from the humaner doctrines of the publicists, more particularly from Vattel, but he never pretends to lay down *authoritatively* the law, which he nevertheless declares in such a form that it is now possible for a student of law to read it and to gain from it a very vivid notion of what a land war in which England was engaged would be like if unhappily it occurred. I will proceed to read to you certain passages from this Manual, taking portions at the same time from other Manuals, and making some remarks as i go on upon the older history of the customs of war of which it treats. I am sorry to say that the British Government has not thought fit to allow it to be published, and therefore I am afraid it cannot

be procured.   It begins with a statement of general
principles.

‘War, properly so called, is an armed contest
between independent nations, and can only be made
by the sovereign power of the State.   In this country
a formal announcement of war is made by a proclamation issued by her Majesty and posted in the City
of London.   The first consequence of this existence
of a state of war between two nations is, that every
subject of the one nation becomes in the eye of the
law an enemy to every subject of the other nation ; for
as every subject is politically a party to the act of his
own Government, a war between the Governments of
two nations is a war between all the individuals of
each nation.   This principle carried to its extreme
limits would authorise the detention, as prisoners of
war, of subjects of one of the hostile parties travelling
or resident in the country of the other at the time of
the outbreak of war, and the confiscation of their
goods.   The exercise, however, of such a right is contrary to the practice of modern warfare, and the
conduct of Napoleon cannot be justified, who on the
outbreak of the war with England in 1803 seized all
the English travelling in France between eighteen and
sixty years of age, and detained 10,000 of them in
prison, where they remained till the peace of 1814.
The usage with respect to goods is to allow the
owners to dispose of them, or leave them to be

claimed by the owners on the restoration of peace.
The expulsion of subjects of the enemy from the
territory of the opposing state is justifiable, and may
be exercised or not according to circumstances.
During the Crimean war Russians were allowed to
reside quietly both in England and France. In the
Franco-German war of 1870 hostile strangers were
required to quit the soil of France within a few days
after they had received notice to quit. On the
other hand, war is not a relation of man to man, but
of state to state, and in itself implies no private
hostility between the individuals by whom it is carried
on. They are enemies only in their character of
soldiers, and not as men. The object of war, politically
speaking, is the redress by force of a national injury.
The object of war in a military point of view is to
procure the complete submission of the enemy at the
earliest possible period with the least possible expenditure of men and money.' 'Wars,' says Lord Bacon,
' are no massacres and confusions, but they are the
highest trial of right, when princes and states, that
acknowledge no superior on earth, shall put themselves
upon the justice of God for the deciding of their controversies by such success as it shall please Him to
give to either side.'

Going back upon this list of general principles, I
must call your attention to the contrast between the
statement that the first consequence of the existence

of a state of war between two nations is that every subject of the one becomes in the eye of the law an enemy to every subject of the other nation, and the proposition that war is not a relation of man to man, but of state to state, and of itself implies no private hostility between the individuals by whom it is carried on, that they are enemies only in their character of soldiers, and not as men.   Several critics in European countries have remarked on this, that the two propositions do not fall in with one another; that the first of them would authorise the killing of women and children, whereas the second reduces war to a contest between professional soldiers.   I think there is some justice in this criticism, that the two propositions belong to different periods of history. The first represents what might have been the theory of law if an attempt had been made to express it at the period of Greek classical antiquity, while the second proposition represents a new theory to which the world has generally advanced.   Many passages which meet us in Thucydides show that in point of fact in the view of the Greeks war must have been thought (if anybody theorised about it) to be waged between the whole of the subjects of one state and the whole of the subjects of another.   There is a passage that recurs frequently, that they killed the men, and the women and children they reduced to slavery. The women and children were in fact considered, as

well as the men, to be in a state of enmity to the
other belligerent state.   I remark here, what many
have remarked as well, that one consequence of the
decay and abolition of slavery was an increase of
bloodshed.   Women and children and occasionally
grown men had a value of their own which supplied
a motive for keeping them alive, and at a later date
bloodshed was, to a certain extent, diminished by the
practice of ransoming ; and there were no bloodier
wars than those which occurred when the practice of
ransoming had just died out.

The next portion of the Manual has for a title :
‘ The means by which war should be carried on ’—
that is to say, the means by which war is as a fact
carried on among civilised and relatively humane
enemies.   The writer says :   ‘ The poisoning of
water or food is a mode of warfare absolutely forbidden ; but the turning off the supply by stopping
convoys of food to the enemy is one of the usual
methods of reducing them to submission.   The use
of poisoned weapons and of weapons calculated to
produce unnecessary pain or misery is prohibited,
on the ground that, as the object of war is confined
to disabling the enemy, the infliction of any injury
beyond that which is required to produce disability
is needless cruelty.’

As to the poisoning of water and food, the best
explanation of its prohibition is that it seems to have

existed from very earliest times. It is quite certain
that both Greeks and Romans thought that the
poisoning of water and food was worthy only of
barbarians. What was the origin of this feeling ? has
been asked by writers of modern days. It may.
have been that the poisoning of water and food was
thought a peculiarly painful mode of inflicting death.
The only poison of great efficacy which seems to
have been known to antiquity, and which indeed was
the base of the subtle poisons employed in the
Middle Ages by the Italians, was arsenic, which no
doubt causes death coupled with the extremest pain.
Or it may have been the idea that poison was not
fair fighting—and this shows itself as a very strong
feeling in very ancient days—that on the whole each
combatant ought to have the means of employing his
skill in resistance.

On the subject of the use of poisoned weapons,
and weapons calculated to produce unnecessary pain
or injury, one of the chief modern reforms of the law
of war has been attempted, and with as much success
as it was possible for it to command. By the Declaration of St. Petersburg, proposed by the Emperor
Alexander II. and signed in 1868 by all the civilised
Powers, the contracting parties agreed to renounce
the use by their forces on land or sea of an explosive
projectile of a weight below 400 grammes—a little
more than fourteen ounces—charged with fulminating

or inflammable matter. I have heard that this provision in the Declaration of St. Petersburg has no
longer its humane effect in consequence of the progress of science, which, I am sorry to say, has often
had the effect of defeating attempts to increase the
area of humanity. It is alleged that the conical
bullets which are universal in modern armament do
in fact cause pain as severe and wounds as incurable
as ever did the explosive bullets which were just
coming in about the year 1868. I am myself in-
competent to meet the objection, but at all events we
must mark that the Declaration of St. Petersburg,
expressing the opinion of the whole civilised world,
declares that the object of war is confined to disabling
the enemy, and lawful usage does not warrant any
state in causing injuries which give more pain than
is necessary for that comparatively humane object.

A further universally accepted rule is as follows:
' Assassination is against the customs of war. Assassination is the murder by treachery of individuals
of the hostile forces. The essence of the crime is
treachery, as a surprise is always allowable, and a
small force may penetrate into the enemy's camp,
despatch the sentinels, take the general officer
prisoner or kill him, without infringing any of the
customs of war or subjecting themselves, if taken, to
be treated otherwise than as prisoners of war. It is
the duty of the enemy to be prepared against a

military surprise, but not to guard himself against the treacherous attacks of individuals introduced in disguise into the camp.'

Assassination began to be regarded with peculiar horror immediately after the Reformation. No doubt it was the murder of William of Orange, more than suspected of having been prompted by the Spaniards, which brought about the fierce denunciations of which it is the subject. There will always, of course, be some danger of this crime being resorted to when a war, as is sometimes the case, appears to depend entirely on the life of one individual—a great states-man or a great general. That was the position of William of Orange, in the opinion of all his Catholic enemies. But it has often been noted that a new feeling had arisen in the interval between the wars of the Reformation and the progress of the greatest war in which this country has ever been engaged. Many writers quote with the strongest approval the action of Mr. Fox when Foreign Secretary. A promising scheme for the murder of the great Napoleon was communicated to him, and he at once made it known in Paris and informed the Emperor of the danger which threatened him. The feeling elicited by this proceeding of the English Foreign Secretary was so strong and has so little decayed, that I think with the writer of the Manual we may safely lay down that assassination is against the customs of war.

He proceeds : ' With the exception of the means above stated to be prohibited, any instruments of destruction, whether open or concealed, partial or widespread in their effects, shells of any weight, torpedoes, mines, and the like, may legitimately be employed against any enemy ; and seeing that the use is legitimate, there is no reason why the officers or soldiers employing them should be refused quarter or be treated in a worse manner than other combatants.   A humane commander will, no doubt, so far as the exigencies of war admit, endeavour to provide that the effect of the explosion of a mine or torpedo should extend to combatants only, but practically no rule can be laid down on the subject. The general principle is, that in the mode of carrying on war no greater harm shall be done to the enemy than necessity requires for the purpose of bringing him to terms.   This principle excludes gratuitous barbarities, and every description of cruelty and insult that serves only to exasperate the sufferings or to increase the hatred of the enemy without weakening his strength or tending to procure his submission.'

I have further to remark on these portions of the Manuals before us, that one of the most curious passages of the history of armament is the strong detestation which certain inventions of warlike implements have in all centuries provoked, and the repeated attempts to throw them out of use by denying quarter to the soldiers who use them.   The most unpopular and detested of weapons was once the crossbow, which was really a very ingenious scientific invention.   The crossbow had an anathema put on it, in 1139, by the Lateran Council, which anathematised *artem illam mortiferam et Deo odibilem.*   The anathema was not without effect.   Many princes ceased to give the crossbow to their soldiers, and it is said that our Richard I. revived its use with the result that his death by a crossbow bolt was regarded by a great part of Europe as a judgment.   It seems quite certain that the condemnation of the weapon by the Lateran Council had much to do with the continued English employment of the older weapon, the longbow, and thus to the English successes in the wars with France.   But both crossbow and longbow were before long driven out of employment by the musket, which is in reality a smaller and much improved form of the cannon that at an earlier date were used against fortified walls.   During two or three centuries all musketeers were most severely, and as we should now think most unjustly, treated.   The Chevalier Bayard thanked God in his last days that he had ordered all musketeers who fell into his hands to be slain without mercy.   He states expressly that he held the introduction of firearms to be an unfair innovation on the rules of lawful war.

Red-hot shot was also at first objected to, but it was long doubtful whether infantry soldiers carrying the musket were entitled to quarter. Marshal Mont Luc, who has left Memoirs behind him, expressly declares that it was the usage of his day that no musketeer should be spared.

The bayonet also has a curious history. No doubt it must be connected by origin in some way with the town of Bayonne, but the stories ordinarily told about its invention and early use seem to be merely fables. No invention added more to the destructiveness of war, as the bayonet turns the musket into a weapon which is at once a firearm and a lance. The remarkable thing about it is, that though known it remained for so long unused. It was Frederick the Great who is said first to have used it generally or even universally among his soldiers. The probability is that the fear of exposing infantry to deprivation of quarter if taken prisoners caused this hesitation in using it. In our own army we have an example of the feeling which the old usage of war on the subject of certain weapons created, in the green uniform of the Rifle Brigade. It seems to have been long doubted whether foot soldiers armed with the early form of rifle would have their lives granted to them if they were taken prisoners; and the green uniform, first used among the olive foliage of Spain and Portugal, was supposed, it is now said untruly, to give a greater protection than clothes of any other colour at a longer distance.

Looking back on this long-continued state of feeling on the subjects of new and destructive inventions, one may perhaps wonder that mines and torpedoes, and particularly the torpedo of our day, have not met with harsher feeling. But the reason why no such attempts as were formerly tried to drive out of use especial weapons are likely hereafter to be seen, is that, in the first place, any art, and especially an art of destruction, is in our day likely to see rapid improvements. We know of no limit to the power of destroying human life ; and when the extension of the area of this power by a professional class has once set in, it is impossible for us to lay down to what lengths it may go or over what time it may extend. The invention proceeds so rapidly that a peculiarly objectionable form of it can rarely be noted and specified. On the other hand, it is a more satisfactory reflection that wars have on the whole become less frequent, and they have also become shorter. Hence the opportunities of observing the widespread and cruel destruction caused by the most formidable class of new warlike inventions are much rarer than they were.

I will proceed to say something on the history of the torpedoes which occupy so much of our attention. I may remark that when it was first invented the torpedo was received with downright execration.

It first made its appearance in the war between the revolted colonies, now forming the United States, and the mother country, and it was then known as the 'American Turtle.' Many attempts to obtain an improved form of it were made during the war between England and France, when Napoleon and his armies were hanging on the coast. The principle of using clockwork had already been invented, but the peace of 1814 put an end for the time to that method of invention, and it was long before the world heard again of the catamaran, as the torpedo was next called.

The epochs in the period of humanitarian progress and voluntary codification which deserve to be identified with the name of the Emperor Alexander II. of Russia are : the Convention of Geneva as to wounded, acceded to by all the European Powers in the course of the years 1864, 1865, and 1866 ; the Declaration of St. Petersburg in 1868 ; and the Conference at Brussels, which filled the greater part of the year 1874. I refer you for the results of both to Halleck's excellent book.

LECTURE VIII.

THE MODERN LAWS OF WAR

IN my last lecture I explained the detestation which newly-invented instruments of war sometimes occasioned in olden days, and of the severity with which soldiers who employed them were sometimes treated. The Manual for the use of officers in the field, on which I am basing these lectures, states the general rule on the subject of new warlike inventions in the following terms :

' With the exception of the means above stated to be prohibited, any instruments of destruction, whether open or concealed, partial or widespread in their effects, shells of any weight, torpedoes, mines, and the like, may legitimately be employed against an enemy ; and seeing that the use is legitimate, there is no reason why the officers or soldiers employing them should be refused quarter, or be treated in a manner worse than other combatants.' The means above stated to be prohibited are poisoning water or food, assassination, and the use of explosive bullets above a

certain weight. It is added that 'a humane commander will, so far as the exigencies of war admit,
endeavour to provide that the effect of the explosion
of a mine or a torpedo should extend to combatants
only, but practically no rule can be laid down on the
subject.'

The latest instance in which mines of an extent
and destructiveness far exceeding the immediate object
were used, was one which attracted but little notice in
this country owing to the distance of the locality at
which the explosion took place. It happened, however,
that in the course of the advance of the Russian
armies through the Tartar countries to the frontier of
Afghanistan a well-known Russian commander, much
beloved and respected, General Skobeleff, found his
progress obstructed by a great fortification erected
by a large tribe of Tartars. This was the fortress of
Akhal Téké, an enormous construction of burnt clay.
It would have taken much time, and cost many lives, to
attack it by any of the recognised methods of capture.
It appeared, however, that the tribe which had erected
this fortress had no conception whatever of a mine, and
Skobeleff passed several weeks before these walls in
excavating mines of an enormous extent. At last, the
besieged having no suspicion that they were likely to
be attacked in any way except that known to them,
the mines were exploded, and the greater part of the
fortress and a vast number of persons inside it were

at once destroyed. The remainder of the tribe received very severe treatment from the successful besiegers, and but a small portion escaped. It is sad to think that this example of warlike severity was set by the general of the Power which, it would be only just to admit, has done most to mitigate the cruelties of war. Skobeleff defended himself on the ground that what he had done was true humanity rather than severity, and that in no other way could a tribe which was not only formidable in war, but had done much to prevent the even temporary establishment of peace in those countries, be reduced. But, no doubt, in all operations of war which are conducted under the eyes of civilised men, who watch them through the press and the telegraph, the practice is stated in these Manuals, that 'a humane commander will, so far as the exigencies of war admit, endeavour to provide that the effect of the explosion of a mine or a torpedo should extend to combatants only ; but practically,' it is cautiously added, 'no rule can be laid down on the subject.' The general principle is—and this is the conclusion of all these writers—that in the mode of carrying on the war no greater harm shall be done to the enemy than necessity requires for the purpose of bringing him to terms. This principle excludes gratuitous barbarities, and every description of cruelty and insult that serves only to exasperate the sufferings or to increase the hatred of the enemy

L

without weakening his strength or tending to produce his submission.

An interesting question for us to ask ourselves is, whether in the future history of warfare there is likely to be any such proscription of weapons through sheer dislike or horror as was common in the Middle Ages. I am myself not convinced but that hereafter there may be a very serious movement in the world on the subject of some parts of the newly-invented armament. Let us just take into our consideration two new inventions, which have shown themselves capable of causing terrific destruction—two new implements of naval warfare, the Ram and the Torpedo. Neither has been extensively tried at present—one hardly at all. At the battle of Lissa in the Adriatic, on the coast of North America during the War of Secession, and also on the western coast of South America, the ram has been tried, and has proved to be an instrument whose effects can hardly be measured. Ships have been sunk in a moment or two by its use. Of the use of the torpedo, however, we have hardly any example. Among military and naval men there is still great controversy as to its effectiveness. Torpedoes during the Russo-Turkish war were laid down in the mouths of the Danube in great quantities, but the Russians had no difficulty in removing them without injury to themselves ; and all over the world it is still a question whether the defence or the attack, as

these writers put it, is the stronger in their case.
In this country, I think, which is confident of the
possession of the most formidable forms of this im-
plement, there is at present considerable belief in
its effectiveness in war ; but in France, on the other
hand, the opinion on the whole tends in the other
direction. French naval writers maintain emphati-
cally that, as yet, it has not been proved that the
torpedo is a weapon which can be used on a large
scale with safety by a naval combatant ; but these
French writers have raised a question which is
extremely interesting to us with regard to the discussion which I am just closing. 'You must remember,' says one of them, a celebrated French
admiral, ' that a torpedo is used under water and in
the dark. Now, are you quite sure that you will
always aim your attack against the ship which you
intend to destroy? Suppose that the commander of a
torpedo fleet makes his way to a force of ships lying
off a particular coast, and one of his torpedoes is
successfully fixed to the vulnerable parts of one of
them. The electric spark is applied, and the ship
and everybody on board it is blown into the air or
sent into the depths of the sea! Supposing, however,
immediately afterwards it is discovered that the ship
which has been destroyed is a neutral, perhaps one of
the finest vessels of a friendly Power! Do not you
think that there would be a thrill of horror through

the civilised world, and are you sure that a combination of civilised nations will not be formed which will
condemn the torpedo to the same proscription, and
perhaps by the same means, as far more merciful
weapons were condemned in the Middle Ages?' For
my part, I think this reasoning exceedingly strong,
and I am not yet convinced that warlike invention
may not reach some point at which the natural
feelings of humanity will cause it to be arrested.

I pass now briefly to a portion of these Manuals
which in spirit is a good deal connected with that
which I am placing before you. It is the chapter
which they contain on ' Spies and Stratagems.' A
spy, they all say, in a military sense is a person who
is found in a district occupied by the enemy collecting secretly, and in disguise, information respecting
his condition and designs, with a view of communicating such information to the opposing force.
Secrecy and disguise are the essential characteristics
of a spy in the military sense. An officer in uniform, however nearly he approaches to the enemy,
or however closely he observes his motions, is not a
spy, and if taken must be treated as a prisoner of
war. Spies when taken are punishable with death,
either by hanging or shooting. The services of spies
must be secured by rewards, as no one can be called
upon to undertake the office of spy as a matter of
duty or against his will. A commander may, of

course, avail himself of information if given by a
traitor. How far he is justified in endeavouring to
suborn treachery, is a more difficult question. Such
transactions are said by Vattel to be not uncommon,
though never boasted of by those who have entered
on them. An officer may feign to be a traitor for
the purpose ef ensnaring an enemy who attempts to
corrupt his fidelity ; but if he voluntarily makes
overtures to the enemy under pretence of being a
traitor, and then deceives the enemy with false information, his conduct is dishonourable, and contrary to the customs of war. Prisoners of war
cannot be punished or ill treated for refusing to dis-
close the number or condition of the body to which
they belong. False attacks, the dissemination of
false information or pass-words when not perfidious,
are permissible by the customs of war. Indeed, to
take a town by surprise, or to turn a position by
a stratagem, is more glorious nowadays to a General
than to effect the object by force, in proportion as to
win a great battle with little slaughter is more creditable to the skill of the General than to gain a bloody
victory. It must, however, be observed that no
deceit is allowable where an express or implied engagement exists that the truth should be acted or
spoken. To violate such an engagement is perfidy,
and contrary alike to the customs of war and the
dictates of honour. For example, it is a gross breach

of faith and an outrage against the customs of war
to hoist a Hospital flag on buildings not appropriated
to the wounded, or to use a place protected by a
Hospital flag for any other purpose than a Hospital.

The opinion here expressed, that successes gained
through a spy are more creditable to the skill of a
commander than successes in drawn battles, was very
largely held in the last century, and military writers
of great celebrity have left accounts of the successful
use which they made of spies and their services.
Frederick the Great of Prussia, in November 1760,
published Military Instructions for the use of his
Generals, which were based on a wide practical knowledge of the matter. He classed spies as 'ordinary
spies,' 'double spies,' 'spies of distinction,' and
'spies by compulsion.' By 'double spies' he meant
spies who also pretended to be in the service of the
side they betrayed ; by 'spies of distinction' he
meant officers of Hussars whose services he found
useful under the peculiar circumstances of an Austrian campaign.   When he could not procure himself spies among the Austrians owing to the careful guard which their light troops kept around their
camp, the idea occurred to him, and he acted on it
with success, of utilising the suspension of arms that
was customary after a skirmish between Hussars, to
make those officers the means of conducting episto-
lary correspondence with the officers on the other

side. 'Spies of compulsion' he explained in this
way. When you wish to convey false information to
an enemy, you take a trustworthy soldier and compel
him to pass to the enemy's camp to represent there
all that you wish the enemy to believe. You also
send by him letters to excite the troops to desertion ;
and in the event of its being impossible to obtain information about the enemy, Frederick prescribes the
following : choose some rich citizen who has land
and a wife and children, and another man, disguised
as his servant or coachman, who understands the
enemy's language. Force the former to take the
latter with him to the enemy's camp to complain of
injuries sustained, threatening him that if he fails to
bring the man back with him after having stayed
long enough for the desired object his wife and
children shall be hanged and his house burnt. ' I was
myself,' he adds, 'constrained to have recourse to
this method, and it succeeded.' The humanity and
good faith of Frederick the Great have never been
celebrated ; but how much of these principles survive
to our own times we can gather from Lord Wolseley's
' Soldier's Pocket Book.' ' The best way,' he suggests,
' to send out a spy is to send a peasant with a letter
written on very thin paper, which may be rolled up
so tightly as to be portable in a quill an inch and a
half long, and this precious quill may be hidden in
the hair or beard, or in a hollow at the end of a

walking stick. It is also a good plan to write secret correspondence in lemon juice across a newspaper or the leaves of the New Testament. It is then safe against discovery, and will become legible when held before a fire or near a red-hot iron. As a nation,' adds Lord Wolseley, 'we are brought up to feel it a disgrace even to succeed by falsehood. The word " spy " conveys something as repulsive as " slave." We keep hammering along with the conviction that "honesty is the best policy," and that truth always wins in the long run. These sentiments do well for a copy-book, but a man who acts upon them had better sheath his sword for ever.'

One of the most important subjects of which the new Manuals treat is the person of the enemy. The enemy, it is laid down, consists of armed forces and of the unarmed population. The first principle of war is that armed forces as long as they resist may be destroyed by any legitimate means. The right of killing an armed man exists only so long as he resists. As soon as he submits, he is entitled to be treated as a prisoner of war. Quarter should never be refused to men who surrender, unless they have been guilty of some such violation of the customs of war as would of itself expose them to the penalty of death ; and when so guilty they should, whenever practicable, be taken prisoners and put upon their trial before being executed, as it is seldom justifiable in a combatant

to take the law into his own hands against an unresisting enemy.   Most of you, I imagine, are aware
that this principle, stated in this broad way, is quite
modern.   Most of us have learnt, when children,
touching stories of the refusal of quarter to garrisons
that had surrendered in our wars of succession with
France.   Many of us remember Froissart's story of
six citizens of Calais whom Edward III. was with
difficulty restrained from hanging for the obstinate
resistance they had made to the siege of their town.
In point of fact, during this war, and the later war
of Henry V. against France, even when the successful General was disposed to be merciful, he generally
reserved a certain number of the besieged, though a
small number, for execution.   When Rouen surrendered to Henry V. the latter stipulated for three of
the citizens to be left at his disposal, of whom two
purchased their lives, but the third was beheaded.
When the same king, the year following, was besieging the castle of Montereau, he sent twenty prisoners
to treat with the Governor for a surrender ; but
when the Governor refused to treat even to save their
lives, and when, after taking leave of their wives
and families, they were escorted back to the English
army, the King of England ordered a gallows to be
erected, and had them all hanged in sight of those
within the castle.   When Meaux surrendered to the
same king, it was stipulated that six of the bravest

defenders should be delivered up to justice, four of
whom were beheaded at Paris, and its commander at
once hanged on a tree outside the walls of the city.
No doubt this severity was due in a great degree to
the hard measure which in those days was always
dealt out to a force which had resisted an attack
when there was no chance of success. And this is
one ground on which the savage practices which
accompanied storms and sieges were explained ; but
it is always to be recollected that in these French
and English wars there was another cause of extreme truculence. In the minds of those who waged
them they were wars of succession, and questions·
therefore of the faith and submission due to a sovereign mixed themselves up with the ordinary considerations of the field. On reading the accounts of
them carefully, the special severities of our Edward
III. and our Henry V. may be seen to be constantly
explained by the successful king's belief that he was
dealing with traitors who had surrendered themselves ;
and in fact it appears to have been the conviction
that the population attacked owed legally fealty to
the General of the army attacking them, which led
specially to the cruelties of these wars, just as a conviction of the lawfulness of the severest punishment
for heresy and infidelity led to the savageness of the
wars of religion. There is no doubt that at present
the Manuals state the practice correctly, that quarter

ought never to be refused to men who surrender, unless they have been guilty of some such violation of
the customs of war as would of itself expose them to
the penalty of death, and when so guilty they should
whenever practicable be taken prisoners and put upon
their trial before they are executed, for it is seldom
justifiable for a combatant to take the law into his
own hands against an unresisting enemy. The point
was one which was largely discussed at the Conference of Brussels, and it was proposed by some of
the delegates that even spies should be no longer
executed when taken, but should always be treated as
prisoners of war.

We come now to portions of these Manuals of
warlike customs which are pleasanter reading. 'The
wounded must not only be spared, but humanity
commands that if they fall into the hands of their
opponents the care taken of them should be second
only to the care taken of the wounded belonging to
the captors. Surgeons and others in attendance on
the wounded, though forming part of the armed forces,
are exempted from the liability of being attacked
unless they divest themselves of their non-combatant
character by actually using arms, in which case they
may be treated as part of the combatant body. The
same amenity and under the same conditions should
be extended to camp followers, and other persons in
attendance on the army but not bearing arms.'

The first and last parts of this paragraph give the results of the Geneva Convention, the furthest point which has at present been reached by humane doctrine in the actual conduct of war. This Convention was signed on August 22, 1864. It states that it was drawn up for the amelioration of the condition of the wounded of armies in the field. I will read you a few of its principal provisions:

'Ambulance and military Hospitals shall be acknowledged to be neutral, and as such shall be protected and respected by belligerents so long as any sick or wounded may be therein. Such neutrality shall cease if the ambulances or Hospitals should be held by a military force. Persons employed in Hospitals and ambulances, comprising the staff for superintendence, medical service, administration, transport of wounded, as well as chaplains, shall participate in the benefit of neutrality while so employed, and so long as there remain any wounded to bring in and to succour.' The persons designated in the preceding article may even after occupation by the enemy continue to fulfil their duty in the Hospital or ambulance which they serve, or may withdraw in order to rejoin the corps to which they belong. Under such circumstances, when those persons shall cease from their functions they shall be delivered by the occupying army to the outposts of the enemy. As the equipment of military Hospitals remains subject to the laws of war, persons

attached to such Hospitals cannot on their withdraw-
ing carry away any articles but their own private
property ; and under the circumstances an ambulance
shall, on the contrary, retain its equipment.   Inhabitants of the country who may bring help to the
wounded shall be respected and remain free.   The
Generals of the belligerent Powers shall make it their
care to inform the inhabitants of the appeal addressed
to their humanity, and of the neutrality which shall
be the consequence of it.   Any wounded when entertained and taken care of in a house shall be considered as a protection thereto.   Any inhabitant who
shall have entertained wounded men in his house
shall be exempted from the quartering of troops, as
well as from a part of the contributions of war
which may be imposed.   Wounded or sick soldiers
shall be entertained and taken care of, to whatever
nation they may belong.   Commanders-in-chief
shall have the power to deliver immediately to the
outposts of the enemy soldiers who have been
wounded in an engagement, when circumstances
permit it to be done, and with the consent of both
parties.   Those who are recognised, after their
wounds are healed, as incapable of serving, shall be
sent back to their country.   The others may also be
sent back on condition of not again bearing arms
during the continuance of the war.   Evacuations,
together with the persons under whose directions

they take place, shall be protected by absolute neutrality. A distinctive and uniform flag shall be adopted for Hospitals, ambulances, and evacuations. It must on every occasion be accompanied by the neutral flag. A badge for the arm shall also be allowed for individuals neutralised ; but the delivery thereof shall be left to the neutral authority. The flag and the badge shall bear a red cross on a white ground.

The conduct of the Hospitals established under the Geneva Convention has been carried on by surgeons, nurses, and military servants, with the greatest self-sacrifice and with the greatest enthusiasm. Nothing, I hope, will ever occur to provoke retrograde measures with regard to so great a reform. At the same time there are some drawbacks, from a military point of view, to the application of the provisions of the Geneva Convention, on which I will say a few words in conclusion. I am told on very excellent authority that it is very difficult to persuade military commanders in the field of the perfect fairness and good faith with which these provisions are carried into action. You may not fire on a Geneva Hospital or ambulance, and yet the Geneva Hospital, with its ambulances and appurtenances, generally kept a good deal in motion, is a very extensive set of structures, and protects a considerable portion of the field from the line of fire. Generals are apt to think, or to persuade

themselves, that the Hospital has been put in a locality
either expressly designed to cover the fire of one party
or another, or to prevent the fire of one party from being
as effective as it might be.   There is, I am persuaded,
a great deal of delusion about these suspicions, delusion unhappily of the nature which is constantly
arising in the minds of men actually engaged in a
deadly struggle.   All that we have a right to say
here is, that the most abundant good faith should be
used in the localisation and use of these beneficent
mitigations of the hardships of war, and that no
punishment would be too severe for an officer, no
matter his rank, who knowingly used them for the
purpose of inflicting warlike injury on an opponent.

LECTURE IX.

RULES AS TO PRISONERS AND QUARTER.

At the close of my last lecture I spoke of the Geneva
Convention of 1864 as the farthest, as well as the
most recent, point of advance reached by a concert of
nations in the attempt to mitigate the inevitable
sufferings of war. International Law, as now understood, contains a number of rules of greater antiquity
having the same object in view. The status of the
prisoner of war is historically descended from the status
of the slave. He represents the class which, as the
Romans put it, had lost liberty, country, and family ;
by capture he had forfeited to the captor all the rights
which he possessed, and was bound to labour at the
order of the captor, and anybody who succeeded the
captor in title, to the end of his life. But as slavery
fell into disrepute and decay chiefly owing to the
influence of the Christian Church, a number of rules
gradually grew up for the purpose of limiting the
power of the captor over the prisoner of war. They
may be described as intended to prevent his being

treated actually as a slave, in the form which they have now taken. In the Manuals which several of the great civilised states have prepared for their officers in the field, it is declared that the object of detaining prisoners of war is to prevent their taking part again in the operations of war. So much restraint, therefore, and no more, should be applied as is sufficient for that purpose. They cannot be compelled to aid their captors in military operations, but they may be employed in any other manner suitable to their condition. The money which they earn by work should be placed to their credit after deducting the expenses of subsistence. A prisoner of war who has committed an offence against the customs of war—such, for example, as stabbing or robbing wounded men—may be considered to have forfeited the character of a prisoner of war, and be punished with death for his crime. The primary obligation to support prisoners of war necessarily lies with the captor, and he should maintain them in a manner suitable to their condition. A prisoner of war, unless he has given a pledge or promise not to escape, is justified in making the attempt ; but if retaken he is not punishable by death, or otherwise, for having made the attempt, as the customs of war do not regard an attempt to escape on the part of a prisoner as a crime. On the other hand, a rising amongst prisoners of war with a view to effect a general escape may be rigorously punished, even with death in the case of absolute necessity, as self-security is the law of the conqueror, and the customs of war justify the use of means necessary to that end. Stricter means of confinement may be used after an unsuccessful attempt to escape. But a prisoner of war cannot be ill treated or punished for refusing to give information as to the forces to which he belonged, or for giving false information.

It has happened in modern days that after great wars, or where communication between the belligerents was possible during them, serious complaints have been made of the imperfect discharge of the obligations imposed by International Law or by usage on a captor holding a captive in duress. At the close of the War of Secession between the Northern and Southern sections of the United States, the Northern armies obtained possession of the person of a Confederate officer who had been in charge of the prisoners taken by the Confederates during the war. He had been accused of barbarous cruelties towards his enemies who were captives, and the Northern army, after a trial which on the other side was charged with every kind of carelessness and irregularity, put him to death by hanging. The English Government was, at the beginning of this century and the end of the last, constantly accused of barbarity towards the French prisoners who were detained in

the hulks at Portsmouth and other ports ; and probably to this day it is a commonplace amongst the
French that this is one of the greatest crimes which
the English have perpetrated against themselves.
England was in reality in great difficulties in providing places of confinement for the prisoners through
the want or scarcity of such places in this country,
and in the last part of the struggle the Emperor
Napoleon I. is now known to have been indisposed
to facilitate exchange of prisoners between the two
countries.   Gathering his vast armies not only from
France, but practically from the whole of the Continent,
he looked with little favour on anything that would
add to the numbers of the British army, which he
believed to be smaller than it really was, or on anything that would increase the extent of his own
overgrown forces.   Still it is probable that both in
the War of Secession, and in the French and English
war at the beginning of the century, too little
tenderness was shown to prisoners ; and I hope that
with the emphatic expressions which are contained
in the new Manuals, and which will henceforward give
the law in the field, there will be no reason in the
future to make a grievance of the treatment of
prisoners of war.   The only complete mitigation of
the misfortune of captivity is, of course, to be found
either in the escape of the prisoner, on which I have
said a few words, or else in some rules which should

authorise his discharge from the captive condition.
In all probability these methods of releasing prisoners
are all descended from the system of ransom now
extinct. One result of the theory that the captive
had become a slave was, naturally, that if he were
able he might pay to his captor such a price as would
induce him to release what had become his own property. Very large sums of money seem to have been
exacted in the Middle Ages as the ransom of a mailed
knight when taken prisoner. He was usually a man
of birth and of wealth ; but as he lost his relative
importance, and as the most effective part of armies
came to consist of the men-at-arms, and afterwards of
mercenary troops carrying a new class of weapons,
a number of rules present themselves which are
intended to facilitate the voluntary discharge of the
bulk of the prisoners. After the battle of Poitiers it
is expressly stated that there were so many prisoners
taken as to make it necessary to discharge the
knights, debiting them with the amount of their
ransom and not at once exacting it; and that the rest
of the captives, whose number was very great indeed,
were exchanged.

Exchange has now become one of the regular
customs of war, and one of the most humane and
beneficial, and much disrepute is usually incurred by
the refusal to admit it. At the same time, while
exchange, says the text of the Manuals which I have

been citing, is the ordinary mode of releasing prisoners of war, a nation is not guilty of any actual breach of the customs of war in refusing to exchange its prisoners, and may detain them to the close of the war. Exchanges of prisoners take place number for number, rank for rank, wounded for wounded, with added conditions for added conditions, such, for instance, as not to serve for a particular period. In exchanging prisoners of war such numbers of persons of inferior rank may be substituted as an equivalent for one of superior rank as may be agreed upon, but the agreement requires the sanction of the Government or of the commander of the army in the field. A prisoner of war is in honour bound truly to state to the captor his rank, and he is not to assume a lower rank than belongs to him in order to cause a more advantageous exchange, nor a higher rank for the purpose of obtaining better treatment.

Prisoners of war are also not infrequently released through pledging their word to observe certain conditions imposed by the captor. A prisoner of war so pledging his word is said to give his parole, and if his parole be accepted by the captor, to be paroled. The usual pledge given with a parole is not to serve during the existing war. This pledge only extends to active service against the enemy. It does not refer to internal service, such as recruiting or drilling recruits, quelling civil commotions, fighting against

belligerents unconnected with the paroling belligerents, or the civil or the diplomatic service on which
a paroled person may be employed.   It is laid down
by the legal authorities that paroling is a voluntary
contract entered into between the parties.   The captor
is not obliged to offer to parole a prisoner of war, and a
prisoner of war cannot be compelled to give his parole,
but may remain a captive.   It is a rule that a list of
the names of officers and men paroled should always
be made in writing and be carefully kept.   It is
further a rule that a prisoner of war has no authority
to pledge himself never again to serve against a particular enemy.   The pledge must be confined to a
limited time, as he cannot divest himself wholly of the
duty which he owes to his sovereign and country.
The right of a prisoner of war to give his parole may
be still further limited by the laws of his own country.
If a prisoner make an engagement which is not
approved of by his own Government, he is bound to
return and surrender himself to the enemy.   As a
general rule the commanding officer has an implied
authority to give his parole on behalf of himself and
the officers and men under his command ; an inferior
officer ought not to give parole either for himself or
his men without the authority of a superior officer,
if such an officer be within reach.   And according to
the English practice a state has no power to force its
subjects to act contrary to their parole ; but how far

it is authorised to refuse such paroles, and to force its paroled subjects back into the enemy's lines, would seem to be in principle doubtful. As a general rule it would appear advisable to admit of the validity of the paroles, but to punish the individuals who have given them contrary to the laws of their country. A recaptured prisoner who has violated his parole may be punished with death ; but the modern practice usually is to abstain from the infliction of death, except in an aggravated case, and to substitute strict confinement with severities and privations not cruel in their nature or degree.

These rules, which tend to ameliorate the condition and hopes of prisoners, are, relatively to the whole history of modern war, of ancient origin.

There is another set of rules, on which I propose to say something, which relate to the treatment of the general population of the enemy's country, and these are among the most modern parts of the International system. They constitute a subject of great interest but of very great difficulty ; and indeed it was the attempt to construct a sort of code on this subject which brought the discussions of the Conference of Brussels to an end, and deprived its results, as a whole, of the authority which they otherwise might have possessed. How the questions involved arose I may perhaps best express in the following way : In all wars waged by armies of the modern type, and especially in the war between France and Germany, there arrives a point at which one side or the other may legitimately think that the campaign has ended favourably for him.   In the Franco-German war we may say that this point was reached as soon as the German armies had invested Paris.   But some of you can remember, and others may have read, what followed.   Léon Gambetta, a principal member of the so-called Government of National Defence, escaped from Paris in a balloon and established a separate or branch Government at Tours.   From that point a new campaign of a new nature may be said to have begun.   Large forces were brought together by Gambetta, consisting chiefly of fragments of other armies which had been stationed in particular localities or had marched westwards after defeat from the Germans, and, besides these, of a great part of the hitherto unarmed population of the country called to his standard under what was called a *levée en masse*. This part of the war was conducted with some success on the part of the French, but it at once gave rise to a large number of new questions as to what should be allowed in the conduct of war.   The principles agreed upon by the Brussels Conference appeared to have been these : The first duty of a citizen is to defend his country, but this defence must be conducted according to the customs of war.   These customs require that an enemy should be able to distinguish

between the armed forces and the general population
of a country, in order that he may spare the latter
without exposing his troops to be attacked by persons
whom he might reasonably suppose to be engaged
only in peaceful capacities. Further, war must be
conducted by persons acting under the control of
some recognised Government having power to put an
end to hostilities, in order that the enemy may know
the authority to which he may resort when desirous
of making peace. In ordinary circumstances, therefore, persons committing acts of hostility, who do not
belong to an organised body authorised by some
recognised Government, and who do not wear a military uniform or some conspicuous dress or mark
showing them to be part of an organised military
body, incur the risk of being treated as marauders
and punished accordingly. So far the delegates at
Brussels may be said to have been reasonably agreed ;
but then the qualifications which follow in the
Manuals which the various Governments have now
circulated show how very far the rules laid down
were from being unanimously accepted or agreed to
be universal. They go on to say : ' No rule, however,
can be laid down which is not subject to great ex-
ceptions. For example, the customs of war do not
justify a commander in putting to death or even in
punishing the inhabitants of a town, after an attack
has ceased, on the ground that they fought against

him without uniform or distinguishing marks, as all the inhabitants of a town may be considered to be legitimate enemies until the town is taken. Similarly a population which rises *en masse* in a country not already occupied by the enemy are entitled to be treated as prisoners of war, and not as marauders, but in such case they must be formed into organised bodies. Again, when the regular Government of a country has been overthrown by civil tumult, the absence of the authority of a recognised Government to make peace would not of itself disentitle organised bodies of men, clearly distinguishable as foes and fighting in conformity with the customs of war against a foreign enemy, to be treated on capture as prisoners of war. Every case must be judged by its own circumstances, having regard to the principle that persons other than regular troops in uniform, whose dress shows their character, committing acts of hostility against an enemy, must, if they expect when captured to be treated as prisoners of war, be organised in such a manner or fight under such circumstances as to give their opponents due notice that they are open enemies from whom resistance is to be expected.

The extreme difficulty of arriving at complete agreement as to a new set of rules on this vexed subject proved insurmountable at the Brussels Conference ; and in point of fact the debates showed that

at the bottom of the discussion the matters at
stake were the differences in the interests of states
who possess such vast armies as served under the
colours of the Germans or the French, and those
smaller states which, either from policy or from
poverty or from smallness, declined or were unable
to keep on foot armies on that scale.   The following
remarks are to be found in the despatch in which
the English Secretary of State, Lord Derby, summed
up the results of this most remarkable controversy.
He says at the fifth page of his despatch, published
in 1875 : ' The second chapter of the report of the
Conference relating to combatants and non-combat-
ants showed an equal difference of opinion, smoothed
over, in the long run, by a compromise.   The Swiss
delegate, in his observations on the article requiring
the use of a distinctive badge, recognisable at a distance, remarked that a country might rise *en masse*,
as Switzerland had formerly done, and defend itself
without organisation and under no command.   The
patriotic feeling which led to such a rising could not
be kept down ; and although these patriots, if defeated,
might not be treated as peaceful citizens, it could not
be admitted in defence that they were not belligerent.'
The English delegate also reported that during the
general discussion on the subject of this chapter the
Netherlands delegate remarked that if the plan laid
down by the German delegate was to be sanctioned,

on the adoption of those articles which relate to
belligerents as drawn up in the project, it would
have the effect of diminishing the defensive force of
the Netherlands, or render universal and obligatory
service necessary—a military revolution to which the
public opinion of the Netherlands was opposed.   He
therefore reserved more than ever the opinion of his
Government.   The Belgian delegate also made a
declaration of reservation.   In the opinion of the
Belgian delegate no country could possibly admit that
if the population of a *de facto* occupied district should
rise in arms against the established authority of an
invader, they should be subject to the laws in force in
the occupying army.   He admitted that in time of
war the occupier might occasionally be forced to
treat with severity a population who might rise,
and that from its weakness the population might be
forced to submit ; but he repudiated the right of any
Government to require the delivering over to the
justice of the enemy of those men who from patriotic
motives and at their own risk might expose themselves to the dangers consequent upon a rising.
The Swiss delegate, who had previously pointed out
that the Conference was now engaged upon the
cardinal points of the whole project, openly declared
that two questions, diametrically opposed to each
other, were before the Commission : the interest, on the
one hand, of great armies in an enemy's country, which

demands security for their communication and for
their *rayon* of occupation ; and, on the other, the principles of war and the interests of the invaded, which
cannot admit that a population should be handed over
as criminals to justice for having taken up arms
against the enemy.   The reconciliation of these conflicting interests was at this period impossible in the
case of a *levée en masse* in the occupied country, and
in the face of the opposite opinions expressed, until a
provisional modification of them was accepted by the
meeting, passing over this point, on which the greatest
disagreement had been shown.

These difficulties, which prevented the project of
the Brussels Conference from becoming part of the
International Law of civilisation, are no doubt to be
attributed to the fact that reminiscences of the great
war between France and Germany dominated the
whole of these debates.   It is one among many
examples of a truth of considerable importance, that
the proper time for ameliorating the critical parts of
International Law is not a time immediately or shortly
succeeding a great crisis.   Hereafter I shall point out
to you some conclusions to which this truth seems to
me to point.

There is another part, however, of International
Law upon which, if it be possible, it is extremely
desirable to have a systematic set of rules.   It is
perhaps an inevitable but certainly a frequent result

of the present want of rules, that when enemies
are fighting in the same country, and one side com-
plains of the measures adopted by the other, there
is no means of punishing what is thought to be
an infraction of rule except retaliation or, as the
technical word is, reprisals. Retaliation, we are told,
is military vengeance. It takes place where an outrage committed on one side is avenged by the commission of a similar act on the other. For example,
an unjust execution of prisoners by the enemy
may be followed by the execution of an equal number of prisoners by their opponents. Retaliation
is an extreme right of war, and should only be resorted to in the last necessity. ' It may be well to
notice,' says the writer I am quoting, incidentally for
the purpose of reprobating it, ' the idea once prevailed that a garrison which obstinately defended a
place when it had, in the opinion of the enemy, become untenable, might be put to the sword.' There
is no doubt that during the Franco-German war
reprisals were carried to unjustifiable lengths on both
sides. The French Government has published a
curious volume which reproduces all the placards
which either they or others had affixed to the walls
during the contest in France. At one point the
Germans granted no quarter during an attack on a
village, on the plea that twenty-five *francs-tireurs*
(riflemen) had hidden in a wood . near it, without any

regular officer or uniform, and had shot down as many Germans as came within range of their guns. On another of these placards is a notice by a French officer to the Prussian commander of Châtellerault in reference to the alleged resolve of the latter to punish the inhabitants of that place for the acts of some of the *francs-tireurs*. 'I give you my assurance, threat for threat, that I will not spare one of the two hundred Prussian soldiers whom you know to be in my hands ' And indeed General Chanzy, himself a gallant officer in high place, wrote to the Prussian commander of Vendôme, and stated that he intended to fight without truce or mercy because it is a question now not of fighting loyal enemies but hordes of devastators.   On this great subject the Brussels Conference was able to do but little except to suggest that retaliation should only be resorted to in the most extreme cases, and should be conducted with the greatest possible humanity.

LECTURE X.

RELATIONS OF BELLIGERENTS ON LAND.

THE Brussels Conference failed to solve a number
of questions of modern origin which have arisen as
to the status of the 'civil population of a country
when, by rising *en masse*, they take upon themselves
military duty in resistance to an invader.   The
trenchant German scheme, which was submitted to the
Conference, failed to command support, and a number
of rules, which were not open to the same objections
as those which the German delegate proposed, were
not universally acceptable.   But, as in the case of
many other recommendations emanating from the
Conference, a large number of their proposals are
found in the Manuals of warfare which so many
civilised Governments have now placed in the hands
of their officers.   As regards the most important
point which had to be settled, there is a general
tendency to advise that a uniform of some kind shall
be adopted by the non-military population, and
that the corps which they form shall be treated

with humanity, and not shot or hanged as mere marauders.

These questions do not become of much practical importance till a large part of the invaded country has been occupied by the forces of the invader. In the former lecture I took the investment of Paris by the German troops as exemplifying the point of a war at which this branch of law assumes a new importance. We have now to consider the legal position of that part of the invaded country which is under military occupation by the enemy. The view of a country in such a position has much changed in modern times. Of old the theory of the position of an invaded country was much affected by the Roman Law. Land, like everything else, might be captured by occupancy (*occupatio*) subject to what the Romans called *post-liminium*, a legal rule which is generally described as embodying a legal fiction under which a citizen who should after captivity return to his country, or property which after capture should fall again into the hands of the restored owner, reverts to his or its antecedent position. Thus territory militarily occupied was regarded as passing to the occupant subject to the ill-defined risks arising from the return of the former sovereign. Frederick the Great, when he had invaded a country, usually compelled the population to supply him with recruits ; and there is one instance in which the King of

N

Denmark sold what were then two Swedish provinces—Bremen and Verden—to Hanover. The inconvenience of this condition of the law was much felt after the close of the Seven Years' War, and the position of a country once invaded, from which the enemy has retired, was always settled by particular treaty. Manifold as have been the variations of boundary in Europe, they are now always regulated by treaty at the end of a war, and even in the East it is now not easy to find territory held by the rights arising from simple conquest. The only instance of a new province held on the mere title of conquest, and incorporated with the other territories of the conquering country, is the Indian province long known as Lower Burmah. The King, who still retained a part of his territories, which he reigned over at Mandalay, refused, even though utterly defeated, to enter into any treaty of cession, and after the second war Lower Burmah was treated as already part of the general Indian territory.

I have said that the most critical moment in great wars of invasion is that at which a large part of the territory is militarily occupied. There is very much on the subject in the modern Manuals of war. The following is a summary of the law.

An invader is said to be in military occupation of so much of a country as is wholly abandoned by the forces of the enemy. The occupation must be real and not nominal, and it is laid down that a 'paper' occupation is even more objectionable in its character and effects than a 'paper' blockade. On the other hand, the occupation of part of a district from the whole of which the enemy has retired, is necessarily an occupation of that district, as it is impossible in any other way to occupy any considerable extent of territory. The true test of military occupation is exclusive possession. For example, the reduction of a fortress which dominates the surrounding country gives military possession of the country dominated, but not of any other fortress which does not submit to the invader. Military occupation ceases as soon as the forces of the invader retreat or advance in such a manner as to quit their hold on the occupied territory. In the event of a military occupation the authority of the regular Government is supplanted by that of the invading army. The rule imposed by the invader is the law of war. It is not the law of the invading state nor the law of the invaded territory. It may in its character be either civil or military, or partly one and partly the other. In every case the source from which it derives its authority is the same, namely the customs of war, and not any municipal law; and the General enforcing the rule is responsible only to his own Government and not to the invaded people. The rule of military occupation has relation only to the inhabitants of the invaded country. The

troops and camp followers in a foreign country
which has been occupied—let us say by the English
army—remain under English military law, and are
in no respects amenable to the rule of military
occupation. As a general rule, military occupation
extends only to such matters as concern the safety of
the army, the invader usually permitting the ordinary
civil tribunals of the country to deal with ordinary
crimes committed by the inhabitants. The course,
however, to be adopted in such a case is at the discretion of the invader. He may abrogate any law in
the country, and substitute other rules for it. He may
create special tribunals, or he may leave the native
tribunals to exercise their usual jurisdiction. The
special tribunals created by an invader for carrying
into effect the rule of military occupation in the case
of individual offenders are usually military courts,
framed on the model and carrying on their proceedings
after the manner of courts-martial; but of course,
technically, courts so established by an English
General would not be courts-martial within the meaning of our Army Acts. The courts would be regulated only by the will of the General. The most
important power exercised by an invader occupying
a territory is that of punishing, in such manner as he
thinks expedient, the inhabitants guilty of breaking
the rules laid down by him for securing the safety of
the army. The right of inflicting such punishment
in case of necessity is undoubted; but the interest of

the invader no less than the dictates of humanity
demand that inhabitants who have been guilty of an
act which is only a crime in consequence of its being
injurious to the enemy, should be treated with the
greatest leniency consistent with the safety and well-
being of the invading army.

The American rules on the subject of the government of armies in the field say : Martial law, or in
other words the law of military occupation, should be
less stringent in places and countries fully occupied
and fairly conquered.   Greater severity may be exercised in places or regions where actual hostilities exist,
or are expected and must be prepared for.   Its most
complete sway is allowed even in the commander's
own country when face to face with an enemy, because of the absolute necessities of the case and of the
paramount duty of defending the country against invasion.   To save the country is of course paramount
to all other considerations.

In conclusion, it must be borne in mind that an
invader cannot, according to the customs of war, call
on the inhabitants to enlist as soldiers or to engage
actively in military operations against their own
country.   The theory in its full sway is this.   In a
country militarily occupied all executive and legislative power passes to the invader.   It does not follow that he exercises these powers, but theoretically
they belong to him.   The Duke of Wellington made
some observations in the English Parliament which

are recognised as authoritative in all the modern Manuals. ' Martial law,' he said, ' is neither more nor less than the will of the General who commands the army ; in fact, martial law means no law at all. Therefore the General who declares martial law and commands that it shall be carried into execution is bound to lay down distinctly the regulations and rules according to which his will is to be carried out. Now, I have in no country carried out martial law ; that is to say, I have not governed a large proportion of a country by my own will. But then what did I do ? I declared that the country should be governed according to its own national law, and I carried into execution my so declared will.' Comparing this state of the law with that from which we started, it is evident that the ancient practice and theory of occupation have much changed. They have not now any connection with Roman Law, nor would any one nowadays think of borrowing the Roman Law for their rules. The modern practice rests, in fact, upon military necessity, and is circumscribed by the military necessity. An invading General can do certain things because, by the hypothesis, there is no one else to do them. In England the legal rule is the same in peace as in war. The soldiery can always be employed in our own country when sufficient necessity can be shown for using them through the temporary or local abeyance of civil authority.

This state of things comes to an end with the cessation of war. Wars do not in our day linger on, as did the old wars of succession and the old wars of religion. There is always within some moderate time a treaty of peace. Indeed, the modern difficulty in closing a war is, sometimes, to find an authority capable of making peace. This difficulty was much felt by the Germans after they had proceeded a great length in their conquest of France in the last war. They made up their minds that the only authority which could make a treaty on the part of France which Frenchmen would respect was a National Assembly, and therefore before making peace they insisted that such an Assembly should be elected.

I think it may be useful to say a few words on the treaties of peace by which war is nowadays brought to an end. In modern times a peace is always preceded by an armistice, and an armistice by a *suspension of arms*, which is only a shorter armistice. The rule laid down by the international lawyers is that a state of war is brought to an end by a treaty of peace or by a general truce. A treaty of peace puts an end to the war and absolutely abolishes the subject of it ; a general truce puts an end to the war, but leaves undecided the question which gave occasion to it. In modern times these general truces have fallen out of use. They were common enough in the Middle Ages, especially between the Turks and their Christian

enemies, because the religion of neither party permitted the combatants to conclude a definite treaty of
peace.   It has always been laid down that treaties and
general truces can only be concluded by the sovereign
power of a state, and not that of any other authority.
An *armistice* is defined as a partial truce. The power
to conclude an armistice is essential to the fulfilment
by the commanding officer of his official duties, and
therefore he is presumed to have such power delegated
to him by his sovereign without any special command.
This presumption of authority is held to be so strong
that it cannot be rebutted by any act of the sovereign.
If an officer makes an armistice in disobedience to
orders received from his sovereign, he is punishable by
that sovereign ; but the sovereign is bound by the
armistice, inasmuch as the enemy could not be supposed to have known of the limitation of authority
imposed on the officer.

It is suggested by several of the international
writers, and it is probable, that armistices first arose
from the truce or truces of God which were repeatedly
proclaimed by the Church.   These truces took many
and very singular forms.   Thus one famous truce of
God was to begin every Wednesday at sunset, and
last till the following Monday at sunrise.   It was to
continue from Advent to the octaves of Epiphany, and
from Quinquagesima Sunday to the octaves of Easter.
If any person broke the truce and refused to give

satisfaction he was excommunicated, and after the third admonition the bishop who excommunicated him was not to admit him into communion under the penalty of deprivation. The truce was confirmed at many councils, and especially at the Lateran Council of 1179. Some of the regulations were extended into England, and Wednesday and Friday were set apart as days for keeping peace. It is exceedingly likely that these temporary and limited truces accustomed the warlike communities of those days to temporary suspensions of hostilities, and armistices manifestly grew into considerable favour. But they also gave rise, and indeed they give rise still, to a number of rather difficult questions. We find a great number of rules laid down as to what belligerent parties might do or might not do during an armistice. The views taken of these duties in modern times are decidedly contra-dictory. On the one side it is held that all equivocal acts of hostility should be abstained from during an armistice whether they come, or do not, within the description of acts capable of being interrupted by the enemy ; while on the other hand it is contended that, according to the practice of modern warfare, belligerents have a perfect right to alter the disposition of their troops, construct entrenchments, repair breaches, or do any acts by which they may think fit to prepare themselves for the resumption of hostilities. The violation of an armistice by either of the contending

parties gives to the other the right to put an end
to it; but its violation by private individuals only
confers the right to demand the punishment of the
guilty persons. The question is one of great practical difficulty, and in all the Manuals the advice is
given that the greatest caution should be observed in
the case of an armistice to specify the acts which are
or are not to be permitted during its continuance.

Another question which, evidently, was thought
to present great difficulties, was the date of the commencement and the time of the termination of an
armistice. Supposing it to be made for a certain
number of days—that is, from the 1st of May to the
1st of August—questions have been raised whether
the days named are both included or excluded.
The usual mode of reckoning in England as legal
time is to include the first day and exclude the last.
Consequently, in the above-mentioned case, according
to English law, the truce begins at the moment on
which the 30th of April ends and ceases at the
moment at which the 31st of July ends. To avoid
difficulties, it should be stated from the 1st of May
inclusive to the 1st of August inclusive, if it is intended to include the 1st of August; or better
still to begin at a certain hour on one day, and to
end at a certain hour on another. In the case of a
short armistice the number of hours should be stated;
and it is advisable in all cases where an armistice has

been arranged, to agree to indicate by some signal—
for example, the hoisting of a flag or the firing of a
cannon—both the commencement and the termination
of the armistice. An armistice, it is to be remembered, is only a qualified peace, and the state of
war continues, though active hostilities are sus-
pended. This anomalous state of things leads, in
the absence of express stipulation, to considerable
difficulty in ascertaining what is allowed to be done
or continued to be done. Apart from particular
stipulation, the general rule seems to be that a
belligerent cannot take advantage of an armistice
to do any aggressive act which but for the armistice
he could not have done without danger to himself.
For example, in the case of an armistice between a
besieging army and a besieged town, the besiegers
must not continue their works against the town, and
the besieged are forbidden to repair their walls, raise
fresh fortifications, or introduce succours or reinforce-
ments into the town. The last dangerous question
which arose in Europe, arose on one of the class of
terms which I have been examining.

Before closing this lecture it will be useful to note
the substance of the statements made in the modern
Manuals in respect to a number of terms which are
in much use in this part of military operations, but
which are very loosely employed by civilians and even
by historical writers. First as to what is called a

Capitulation.   A capitulation is an agreement for
the delivery of a besieged place or forces divided in
the field into the hands of the enemy.   The commanders on either side are invested with power to
agree to the terms of a capitulation, inasmuch as the
possession of such powers is necessary to the proper
exercise of their functions.   On the other hand, the
extent of their powers is limited by the necessity for
their exercise.   In the surrender of a place the questions at issue are the immediate possession of the place
itself, and the fate of the garrison.   A capitulation,
therefore, must be limited to these questions.   It may
declare that the garrison is to surrender uncondition-
ally as prisoners of war, or to be entitled to march
out with all the honours of war.   It may also provide
that the soldiers comprising the garrison are not to
serve again during the war.   Further conditions for
the protection of the inhabitants and of their privileges, and for their immunity from pillage or contri-
bution, may fairly be put into a capitulation.   A
stipulation in a capitulation to the effect that the
garrison should never again bear arms against the
forces of the conquering state, or that the sovereignty
of the town should change hands, would be invalid,
inasmuch as powers for such extensive purposes
belong only to the sovereign power of the State, and
cannot ever be presumed to be delegated to inferior
officers.

A few words will not be thrown away on Flags of

Truce. Such a flag can only be used legitimately for the purpose of entering into some arrangement with the enemy. If adopted with a view surreptitiously to obtain information as to the enemy's forces, it loses its character of a flag of truce and exposes its bearer to the punishment of a spy. Great caution, however, and the most conclusive evidence are held to be necessary before the bearer of such a flag can be convicted as a spy. The bearer of a flag of truce, at the same time, should not be allowed without permission to approach sufficiently near to secure any useful information. When an army is in position, the bearer of a flag of truce should not, without leave, be permitted to pass the outer line of signals, or even to approach within the range of their guns.

When a flag of truce is sent from a detachment during an engagement, the troop from which it is sent should halt and cease firing. The troop to which it is sent should, if the commander is willing to receive it, signal to that effect and also cease firing; but it must be understood that firing during an engagement does not necessarily cease on the appearance of a flag of truce, and that the parties communicating with such flags cannot complain if those who sent them should carry on the firing. When it is intended to refuse admission to a flag of truce, the bearer should, as soon as possible, be signalled to retire; and if he do not obey the signal, he may be fired upon.

A few words may be usefully added on other

terms of the art of war which are allied to those which I have been defining.   A Cartel is an engagement for the exchange of prisoners of war.   A cartel ship is a ship commissioned for the exchange of prisoners. She is considered a neutral ship, and must not engage in any hostilities or carry implements of war except a signal gun.   A Safe-conduct or Passport is a document given by the commander of a belligerent force enabling certain persons to pass, either alone or with servants and effects, within the limits occupied by the force of such commanding officer.   In the so-called Schnabele case which arose on the frontier of France and Germany, you may remember, it was decided there might be an implied safe-conduct.   The expression 'passport' is usually applied to persons, and 'safe-conduct' both to persons and things.   A safe-conduct for a person is not transferable, and comes to an end at the date stated, unless the bearer is detained by sickness or other unavoidable cause, in which case it terminates on the cessation of the cause.   A safe-conduct may be revoked if it is injurious to the State ; that is, an officer preparing for a great expedition may revoke the safe-conduct of a person who would by means of such safe-conduct be able to carry information to the enemy.   In such case, however, he must give time and opportunity to the bearer to withdraw in safety. A safe-conduct, however, for goods admits of their being removed by some person other than the owner,

unless there is some specific objection against the
person employed. A Safe-guard is a guard posted
by a commanding officer for the purpose of protecting property or persons against the operations of his
own troops. To force such a guard is by English
law a military offence of the gravest character, and
our Army Act makes it punishable by death.

You may remember that not many months ago
serious uneasiness was felt throughout Europe on
account of an incident on the new French and German
frontier. A French official, belonging by birth to the
former German population of provinces now French,
was found on territory now German, under circumstances which made him liable to arrest under a
German law. His defence was, that on that and
several past occasions he had been invited by the
German frontier officials to help in settling border
questions. The German officials asserted that, however that might be, he was on the present occasion
engaged in acts of hostility to Germany. After some
diplomatic correspondence, the German Government
laid down that, if German officials invited a French
functionary to cross the frontier into German territory
for any reason, he enjoyed an implied safe-conduct to
his home in France, and therefore M. Schnabele was
released. The controversy, therefore, ended in the
establishment of the point that a safe-conduct may be
not only express but implied.

LECTURE XI.

RIGHTS OF CAPTURE BY LAND.

BEFORE I leave the group of subjects discussed in the more recent lectures, it may be well to say something on a branch of the law of war by land which tries to regulate incidents of belligerency that cause sometimes as much suffering and very constantly more irritation than actual hostilities. This is the law of the capture of property in land war. I said in a former lecture that a war by land resembles a maritime war in the principles which are applied to the capture of property ; but there is a great practical difference between the two, if neutrals do not happen to be interested in the same way in wars by land in which they have interest as in wars by sea, since there are no prize courts to insist on regularity and moderation. The principle of capture is that movable property, captured either on land or at sea, is acquired by reduction into firm possession. Leaving, however, movable property for the moment, and passing to immovable, I begin by stating that there is

a great deal on this subject in the older law books. ' A
complete title to the land of a country,' says the leading rule, ' is usually acquired by treaty or by the
entire submission or destruction of the state to which
it belongs.' Here what is meant is the sovereignty
or supreme right over property sometimes called
dominium eminens, the right in the sovereign, whether
corporate or single, to affect property by legislation.
In some rare cases the proprietary right, generally in
private hands, cannot be separated from the eminent
domain. This occurs in India, and more or less,
probably, all over the East. The sovereign is the
universal proprietor ; but in our day the quasi-proprie-
tary rights which a conquered sovereign has created
or respected, would in practice be maintained by a
successful invader. Such, in fact, was the case in the
recent British conquest of Burmah proper. But in
the older International Law books another kind of acquisition by capture of private property in land seems
to be chiefly contemplated. The writers appear to be
thinking of the seizure of land which is private
property by the soldiers of the conquering and invading army, much in the same way in which the
provinces of the Roman Empire are supposed to have
been taken possession of by the Teutonic barbarians.
Nowadays that is a case which never practically
occurs ; but if it happened, the occupant of the land
would hold it subject to the Roman principle of post-

O

liminy. If the former owner returned he would revert to his old rights, and the new owner would be ousted. A more conceivable case is one in which an occupying civilian should sell for value a portion of the land of which he has taken possession. Here, too, in theory the principle of post-liminy would intervene, but the result would be that every sale of captured private property would produce a title to it so bad that one can hardly conceive its being effected. The modern usage is that the use of public land and public buildings, and the rents and other profits accruing from such lands and buildings, form part of the spoils of war. As regards private property in land, belligerents in modern times usually abstain, so far as is consistent with the exigencies of operations of war, from exercising the extreme right conferred by war of seizing or injuring private property or land. This custom obtains only so long as not only the owners, but also the community to which they belong, abstain from all acts of hostility, as it is not unusual for an invader to take or destroy the property of individuals by way of punishment for any injury inflicted by them or by the community of which they are members on the property which he owns. In such cases the innocent must necessarily suffer for the guilty, but a humane General will not, except in a very extreme case, destroy a village for an outrage committed by an inhabitant of that village, or ravage a district to punish an attack made within its limits by a body of marauders. From the powers which a successful enemy enjoys to appropriate land and buildings, it is to be observed that the modern usages of war except museums, churches, and other monuments of art ; and by some it is contended that no public building can be destroyed unless used for belligerent purposes.

If we now turn back to movable property, it is held that the arms, implements of war, and every description of movable property belonging to the State may be taken possession of by an invader. An exception to the right of seizure of movables of the enemy is made, indeed, in the case of archives, historical documents, and judicial and legal records. An invader can hold them so long as he remains in the country and requires their use ; but to take them away with him is an act of barbarism prohibited by the customs of war, for the retention of such documente can by no means tend to put an end to a war, while it inflicts a great and useless injury on the country to which they belong, and specially to those countries, now numerous, which, unlike England, have complete registration of titles to land. The seizure of scientific objects, of pictures, sculptures, and other works of art and science belonging to the public, has derived some sanction from the repeated practice of civilised nations, but would seem incompatible with

the admitted restrictions of the rights of war, which
deprive an enemy of such things only as enable him
to make resistance, and therefore can only be justified
as a measure of retaliation.   Seventy years ago the
question of the right of a successful enemy to carry
away with him works of art was a matter of violent
controversy in this country and in the whole of Europe,
and the subject was several times debated in the
British Parliament.   It is a fact very generally
known that after the early and astonishing successes of
Napoleon Bonaparte in 1796, and afterwards in 1797,
there was only one of the small Italian States which
was not compelled to give up to the conquering
French Government the works of art that were the
glory of its chief cities.   The Apollo Belvedere, the
Dying Gladiator, the Medicean Venus, the Laocoon,
the Bronze Horses, were conveyed to Paris and de-
posited in the Louvre, in which they remained until
the overthrow of the first French Empire.   On the
overthrow of that Empire, when the allies, entering
Paris for the second time, gained possession of the
whole city, they restored most of these famous master-
pieces to their original owners.   The French expressed,
and no doubt genuinely felt, the greatest indignation,
which was, however, manifestly treated with much
scorn by the English writers of that day, who seemed
to look upon the anger of the French or Parisian
population as amounting to an absurd refusal to have a

rule applied to themselves which they had freely
applied to others ; but if we are to suppose that strict
law applied to the case there was something to say
against the international validity of the restorations
in the way in which they were actually accomplished.
Arguments, founded on this, were submitted to the
British House of Commons, especially by the great
lawyer Romilly. It was a fact that some of these
works of art had formed part of forced military contributions, which a conqueror may always levy, and
some were given up under express conventions to
which the surrendering state had no power of resistance. In some other cases the state to which the
return was made had been absorbed in another state
during the long war with France. For example,
Venice, which had surrendered some of the most
beautiful works of art in the Louvre, had now become
absorbed in the Austrian Empire. It was further
argued that it was for the advantage of civilisation
that these works of art should not be dispersed over a
number of small cities in Italy which were not then,
all of them, easily accessible, but that they should
remain in a place which on the whole was so easily
reached as Paris. The fact seems to be that the carrying off of these works of art from their old Italian
homes had been a new rule of war. For example,
Frederick the Great, who more than once occupied
Dresden, always spared the famous gallery and its

contents.　The new rule was introduced by Napoleon
Bonaparte as conqueror of Italy, and what the allies
in occupation of Paris applied seems to have been the
rule of reprisal.　There was, no doubt, if we throw
the technical rule aside, a great deal to be urged on
behalf of giving back these sculptures and paintings
to the Italian cities.　They were valued by them more
than any mere property.　Some of these cities before
the war were hardly ever visited except by persons
desirous of seeing some famous work.　As I say, the
one tenable argument against their restoration was
the greater convenience to the civilised world of their
being left in Paris ; but in an age of railways their
distance in Italy is no appreciable inconvenience, and
the Manuals published recently by civilised states
generally condemn the capture of works of art.　Our
own Manual says that the seizure of scientific objects
and works of art can only be justified as a measure of
retaliation.　Here I may observe that an act attributable to a British commander of British troops, which
is almost universally condemned in the numerous
American works on International Law, can always be
justified in the same way.　Undoubtedly, at first sight,
the destruction of the Capitol at Washington in 1814
is not an act of which an Englishman can be proud ; but
on examining the history of that war, it will appear
that the British troops in Washington had been fired
at from the arsenal ; and that also, a short time be-

fore, the chief city of Lower Canada, then called York, had been burnt with all its public buildings by the American troops who occupied it.   Hence this act, which at first sight deserves unqualified condemnation, may be to a certain extent justified as a measure of reprisal.

In all modern books on this subject there is more or less distinct condemnation of unauthorised pillage by the soldiers of an invading army ; yet there is, unfortunately, no doubt that in all wars pillage does continue, and especially in every land war.   There is a very old association between war and pillage, and pillage is generally very easy.   A great deal of it, though not of the worst kind, unquestionably took place when the Germans occupied large portions of France.   The English in Spain abstained from it so far as the orders of Wellington compelled them to do so.   He in fact sometimes employed the severest punishments for the purpose of deterring his troops from plunder ; however, he was operating in a friendly country, and would have suffered serious damage by its being converted to unfriendliness.   A commander may, however, authorise pillage ; but as to authorised pillage there is one considerable mitigation.   Movable property captured according to the Roman principle, which International Law inherited, is *res nullius* ; and it has been several times observed, by myself among others, that in the change of Europe

from Roman to Feudal principles *res nullius* appeared
to have become vested in the sovereign, and very often
in the lord of the manor in which they were found,
and lost therefore their old Roman character.   The
principle obtains in authorised pillage.   It becomes
technically the property of the Crown ; it is collected
together, and then equitably divided among the conquering troops as booty.   It is also to be noted
that modern usage authorises requisitions and forced
military contributions, and, on the whole, the present
theory is that these military contributions and requisitions have superseded all the older forms of capture.

Requisitions may be made in three ways.   First,
the inhabitants may be required to provide supplies
without payment ; secondly, they may be required
to provide supplies at a moderate cost, without regard
being had to the increased value accruing from the
presence of the army ; thirdly, they may be required
to provide the supplies on payment of such price as
they demand.   Which of these three ways is to be
adopted, is in the discretion of the General.   Wellington disapproved of forced requisitions whenever they
could be avoided ; and when he entered France he sent
the Spaniards back rather than be compelled to resort
to requisition for the purpose of supporting his army.
Both the Germans and the French have constantly
exercised the right ; and undoubtedly the strict rule
admitted by the customs of war is that war may

be made to supply itself. The same principles apply to contributions of money levied on a town or on a whole community. As an arrangement such a levy is just, as a means of maintaining an army it is lawful, and possibly in some cases it is more equitable than requisition. The question is, whether it is expedient. It will be very generally remembered that at the close of the Franco-German war an enormous requisition was exacted from the French. The German policy was, undoubtedly, so to cripple France that it should be incapable of further attack on its neighbours. But the money requisitioned for the payment was raised by loans with surprising facility, and it is doubtful whether the enormous increase of the French National Debt—now the largest in the world—which it entailed has seriously affected the feeling of the French people towards those who invaded them.

This subject of foreign loans brings me to a question which has excited perhaps more interest than all other modes of impoverishing an enemy by capture, and one even more important than was at first supposed. Can a sovereign confiscate debts? Can he compel his own subjects, or any community over whom he has military powers, to pay to him debts which they owe to the enemy; that is, to the hostile sovereign or his subjects? The question has been much considered by two high authorities—the

Supreme Court of the United States, and the famous
American jurist Chancellor Kent. The Supreme
Court has solemnly decided that in strict law the
right to confiscate debts still exists as a settled and
undoubted right of war, recognised by the Law of
Nations, but the Court at the same time admitted it to
be the universal practice at present to forbear to seize
and confiscate debts and credits even in a country on
the opening of a war. The Court would not confiscate
any debt without an act of the legislative power declaring its will that such property should be condemned. After a full examination of all the authorities and decisions on this question, Chancellor Kent
says : ' We may, therefore, lay it down as a principle
of public law, so far as the same is understood and
declared by the highest judicial authorities in this
country, that it rests in the discretion of the legislature of the Union by a special law for that purpose, to
confiscate debts contracted by our citizens and due to
the enemy ; ' but it is asserted by the same authority :
' This right is contrary to universal practice, and
therefore it may well be considered as a naked and
impolitic right, condemned by the enlightened conscience and judgment of modern times.'[1] In the
modern instances in which the right has been exercised, it is worth observing that the question of belligerent right was mixed up with the question of allegiance.

[1] Kent, *Comm.* i. 64.

For example, private debts were confiscated as against the Southern States by the Northern States in the war, and by the Southern as against the Northern. And the same principle has a few times been applied in India in a case where the enemy was also a rebel.

But the branch of this question which has now been considered for more than one hundred years is less general than that which I have put ; it is, can a city, can a sovereign, confiscate debts due from itself or himself to enemies ? This is the point raised in the famous case of the Silesian loan. The history of it is as follows : A loan of 80,000l. had been advanced by subjects of Great Britain to the Emperor Charles VI. on the security of the Duchy of Silesia. Silesia, in course of time, was transferred to Prussia by virtue of the Treaties of Breslau and Dresden, and in consideration of this cession Prussia was to discharge the debt. The King of Prussia, however, attached, i.e. took into his own hands, the debt by way of reprisals, but this by the terms of the treaty he had no power to do. He professed himself to be aggrieved by the decision of certain English prize courts in respect of acts of vessels belonging to his subjects, and refused to pay the British subjects the interest which he had pledged himself to pay. The English Secretary of State at once addressed to him, for Prussia was a friendly Power at the time, a letter dated February 8, 1753, in which he dwells upon the unprecedented

nature of the proceeding, and states that he has the
King's orders to send to the King of Prussia a report
made to his Majesty by Sir George Lee, Judge of the
Prerogative Court ; Dr. Paul, his Majesty's Advocate-
General ; Sir Dudley Ryder, and Mr. Murray—the
Mr. Murray who afterwards became Lord Mansfield.
The report in question is one of which British lawyers
and the British Foreign Office have always been exceedingly proud. It is praised by two great foreign authorities of the time—Vattel and Montesquieu ; they both
of them speak of it as admirable ; it is, in fact, a most
excellent example of the method of reasoning of which
International Law admits ; and in the end the King of
Prussia gave way to its arguments, and the interest on
the Silesian loan was ever afterwards punctually paid.
The point which I have been describing is not strictly
raised by the facts, as Mr. W. E. Hall observes in his
book ; but the opinion of the law officers goes into
many questions besides the main question submitted
to them, and among these the trivial question whether
a sovereign can confiscate debts due to himself, and
argues against it. Ever since, it has been held that
no sovereign can under these circumstances refuse to
pay the interest on a loan which he has contracted because the recipients of the interest are for the moment
his enemies. The danger introduced by the Prussian
pretension was a great one. Perhaps we do not
always notice sufficiently the extent to which British

financial and economical interests are bound up with
the sanctity of foreign loans. From the time at which
this country began to grow rich till it became the
richest in Europe, the difficulty of finding investment
for British savings was very seriously felt. In Stuart
times the surplus wealth which was not expended in
land, or embarked directly in trade or manufacture,
which were still in their infancy, was lent on personal
or landed securities. There are plenty of allusions in
the dramatic literature of the seventeenth century
which might be produced in proof of this. It was
scarcity of public investments which led to the violent
struggle between the two companies formed for trading with India which were afterwards fused into the
great East India Company, and also to the hot contest
about the foundation of the Bank of England. In another way this scarcity led to the enthusiasm for mere
speculative undertakings, or, as they were then called,
for Bubbles, such as the South Sea and Darien Companies. During the eighteenth century British savings
were invested in foreign loans wherever they could be
found, as this case of the Silesian loan shows, and probably a good deal of British wealth was embarked in
the constant loans raised by the King of France, who
however, was at all times a very unpunctual debtor.
But the favourite fields, no doubt, during that century
for British investment were the tropical colonies
which were gradually acquired in the West Indies and

more southerly parts of North America. At the end
of that century and in the beginning of the present the
English National Debt grew to such proportions as to
swallow up all other fields of investment ; but at the
close of the great war loans to foreign states became
commoner, and much British wealth was drawn to
them. In early days they had to encounter many
dangers. The various American States had borrowed
largely, but also repudiated largely their liability on
technical grounds. But if a sovereign could have got
rid of indebtedness by going to war with the country
in which he had most creditors, the risk would have
been so great that probably few or no foreign loans
could have been negotiated, and the economic history
of England and Europe would have been quite different. The method of distributing the surplus capital
of the richest countries, to which the civilised world
is greatly indebted, owes its existence to this report
of the English law officers in this deservedly famous
case of the Silesian loan.

LECTURE XII.

PROPOSALS TO ABATE WAR.

In this last lecture of the present course, it seems to me desirable that I should briefly notice some assertions or suggestions, not uncommonly heard in the present day, that the great evils of war might be abated by the adoption of principles of action not necessarily identical with those which have been discussed in previous lectures. I pass over general statements which seem to me to be mere calumnies, such as the charge against influential military men, that in every society they do their utmost to encourage the spirit of belligerency. Those who have had the privilege of acquaintance with famous soldiers will bear me out in saying that, while there is no class of men more humane, there is none distinguished by a deeper dislike or hatred of war, however they may believe it to be inevitable. But another assertion frequently made is much more respectable, and contains a larger proportion of truth. War, it is said, is irreconcilable with Christian belief and Christian practice. If men acted up to the standards of conduct which great

numbers of them theoretically accept, there would be
few wars or none.   This has long been the doctrine
of a sect whose various services to humanity I have
already gratefully commemorated — the Quakers ;
and also óf an obscurer community, the Mennonites.
It will be evident, I think, to everybody who bestows
some careful thought on the subject, that there would
be great difficulty in adapting a system which pro-
fesses to regulate the relations of individual men with
one another, to the relations of groups of men, of
states ; and in point of fact the Quakers have not
always been quite consistent in the application of
their principle.   The Quakers of the colony of
Pennsylvania were in the American War of Independence strong partisans of the colonial cause ; and
Benjamin Franklin has left us some curious stories
of the fictions by which the Pennsylvanian Quakers
reconciled their conscientious objections to war with
their keen desire to assist the colonial troops.   But
it is proper to observe that this opinion of the unlawfulness of war has, in the course of ecclesiastical
history, seemed several times likely to become the
opinion of the whole Christian Church, or of a large
portion of it.   We have most of us been taught to
believe, on the authority of a well-known passage in
Tertullian, that the Roman Imperial armies were full
of Christian soldiers ; but the passage is inconsistent
with others in the same writer ; and I have seen a

long catena of extracts from patristic authorities, extending from Justin Martyr to Jerome and Cyril, in which the inconsistency of the military profession with Christian belief is maintained. In fact, this became one of the main points of contention between Christians and pagans. The contention of Celsus, that the Christians refuse to bear arms even in cases of necessity, is met by Origen with the admission that the fact is so, but with the argument that the Christians do not go on campaigns with the Emperor because they serve him with their prayers. If these opinions did not become those of the whole Church, the cause must probably be sought in the course of historical events, for the invading Teutonic tribes who spread over the Empire could not be untaught the art and practice of fighting, even when they accepted some form of Christianity. Passing over a long space of time to the beginning of the modern history of Christianity, it seemed not improbable that the unlawfulness of war would become a doctrine of all the Protestant sects ; among theologians not quite estranged from Catholicity, the great Erasmus wrote as strongly of the wickedness of war as any Quaker of our day could do, and Sir Thomas More charged Luther and his followers with wishing to deprive sovereigns of their authority by denying to them the power of resistance. On the other hand, the writers

P

dealt with in the foregoing lectures, the founders of
International Law, did not adopt the opinion of
the unlawfulness of war, though they were nearly
all Protestants.   Grotius argues vehemently against
it, chiefly on Scriptural grounds.   I take the fact to
be that he and his immediate followers conceived
the body of rules which they believed themselves to
have rescued from neglect to be more serviceable
for the purpose of regulating the concerns of nations
in war and peace, than any system which pretended
to a direct descent from Christian records or Christian
tradition.   The Law of Nature which they spoke of,
and apparently believed in, with as little hesitation
as if they were thinking of the English Common
Law, has not stood against the assaults of modern
criticism, and specially not against the inferences suggested by the modern study of primitive mankind.
But it did prove possible to apply the rules associated
with it to human societies in peace and war ; whereas,
though a general belief that war was unrighteous
would assuredly have had important effects, nobody
can say confidently what those effects would have
been, or can assert that they would have included
the extension and stability of peace.

Another sweeping proposal for the virtual abolition of war, one of a very different order, however,
from that just considered by me, must have come
under the notice of most of us.   It is said that there

is always an alternative to a contest in arms. Nations fight because they cannot go to law. The old idea that the disputes of states are referred by war to a supernatural arbitrament is now abandoned; but though there is no international tribunal which can entertain as of right the controversies of nations, there is a substitute for it in international arbitration. Let, therefore, every dispute be referred to an arbitrator or to a body of arbitrators, and let civilised communities defer to the award with no more demur than they exhibit in submitting to the decision of a court of justice. A belief in this remedy for war is being widely extended in our day. It is held by persons worthy of all respect and promoted by powerful voluntary associations. I should be the last person to deny that arbitration in international affairs has often been very happily applied. Nations very often, like men, adhere to their view of disputed points more from pride of opinion than from any real interest in it. Some of these disputes, again, turn on questions of fact, which have not been solved because they have not been properly investigated, but which are easily disposed of when thus looked into by fresh and dispassionate minds.

But before this or any other country commits itself to arbitration as a universal remedy for war, one or two of its defects ought to be specially noticed. In the first place, though arbitration in individual disputes is well known and frequently tried, it is very unlike the arbitration proposed by its advocates for international differences.   The arbitration with which all lawyers are familiar, is merely a displacement of the structure of an ordinary court of justice.   The parties agree to refer all or part of the matters in dispute between them to the decision of an arbitrator, who takes the place of the judge or of the judge and a jury, and they at the same time agree that his decision, unless impeachable on certain grounds of law, shall be enforced by the court as would be its own decree.   It is a very convenient course when the questions of fact to be adjudicated upon are numerous and complicated, and the principal objection to it is that it is apt to be very expensive. What I wish to point out is that arbitration as in use between individuals in England does not exclude the one great feature of a court of justice, the force which underlies its operations.   There are, no doubt, arbitrations which come nearer the arbitrations contemplated by the enthusiasts for universal arbitrations between disputant sovereigns.   A skilful man of business in British commercial cities, an eminent specialist in the practical applications of science, will sometimes obtain a sort of celebrity for just and wise adjudication, and nothing like the process of a court is found necessary to secure obedience to his award. It is, however, many centuries since such authority was attributed to any man or class in international matters ; the current of opinion in our day runs distinctly against the assumption that any exceptional knowledge is necessary for the solution of great political and international questions, and therefore the arbitration of which we hear so much would in the long run, and if tried on a great scale, prove to have the defects which would soon show themselves in a court of justice which the State had failed to invest with irresistible coercive power.

The want of coercive power is, in fact, the one important drawback which attends all attempts to improve International Law by contrivances imitated from the internal economy of states, by something like legislation, and by something like the administration of law by organised tribunals.   Still, nobody who understands the subject, and has observed the course of events, will deny a certain measure of success to international arbitrations, and there is much reason to wish them an extended sphere.   But there are some practical defects in them, as they stand, which should be observed upon, because they may possibly admit of being remedied.   It is well known to English practising lawyers that a certain class of litigants are, so to put it, unpopular in English courts, so that there is considerable difficulty in obtaining for them a full measure of justice.   Among these, to give instances, are insurance companies, and to some extent railway companies. In the same way there are states bringing their controversies before bodies of international arbitrators who are in the same sense unpopular litigants ; and, if inquiry were practicable, I should not be surprised to find that, in the opinion of English diplomatists and statesmen in charge of our foreign affairs, our own country is not a popular litigant in arbitrations. The truth is, our country is thought to be very wealthy, and to be able to bear the burden of a money award against it better than any other community. It is believed to be comparatively careless of its foreign policy, and not to show much sensitiveness under a judicial rebuff. Lastly, there is a general impression that it has so contrived its international relations as to escape from its fair share of the anxieties and sufferings which fall upon other states through war, apprehension of war, and preparation for war.

Again, it is not, I think, to be denied that the composition of courts (if I may for the moment so style them) of international arbitration is not altogether satisfactory. An indispensable element in it is one or more of the class of lawyers who are commonly called jurists. But this word has much changed its meaning. As lately as the last century there was a class of lawyers bearing this title who had made a special study of International Law, and whose collective opinion had serious influence on the development of the system. But in England the Ecclesiastical and Admiralty Courts have been transformed, and the special class of lawyers trained in Roman Civil Law who practised in those courts has either disappeared or is on the point of disappearing. Nobody can quite say at present what a jurist is. The word is used in a number of new senses ; and in point of fact most famous foreign writers on International Law are salaried functionaries of foreign chanceries, nor can any reader of very modern treatises on the subject fail to see that many of them are strongly affected by the official connection of the writer with his Government, and by his knowledge of the interest which he supposes that Government to have in the establishment, maintenance, or development of particular features of the international system. This last-mentioned drawback on the usefulness of international quasi-courts of arbitration, that in our day they are not always satisfactorily constituted, is closely connected with one general defect which at present characterises them—they do not exercise any continuous jurisdiction, they are always formed for the single occasion. It is quite uncertain what weight is to be attached to the award of international arbitrators as a precedent. The mode in which International Law makes progress in default of a regular Legislature is a very important subject, which I have not been

able to take up in a manner worthy of it in the
present course of lectures, but which I hope to enter
upon at some future time. There is, however, no
doubt that a quasi-judicial award, given on a serious
occasion, and acquiesced in by powerful nations who
were parties to the litigation, deeply and permanently
affects the law. But quasi-courts of arbitrators, constituted *ad hoc*, of necessity attend simply to the
question in immediate dispute, and do not weigh the
opinion they give regarded as a precedent. They
cannot look before and after—to the entire history of
the Law of Nations. This result of their defective
structure is particularly conspicuous and particularly
dangerous in what was perhaps the greatest of all
arbitrations, that which settled the difference which
had arisen between Great Britain and the United
States as to liability for the depredations of Southern
Confederate cruisers on Northern American shipping.
I have nothing to say against the value of the Geneva
arbitration in regard to the particular occasion on
which it was resorted to. It put an end to a number
of bitterly disputed questions which had accumulated
during the War of Secession, and which might have
smouldered on for years, to the great danger of the
whole civilised world. But the serviceableness of
the Geneva award in its effects on International Law
is much more questionable. Even at the outset, the
disputants are found arguing that the arbitrators

should have regard to principles which one of them
did not admit to be included in International Law.
Great Britain protests against this principle, but
nevertheless allows the arbitration to proceed. We
may, however, be quite sure that if an analogous
dispute should hereafter occur, this principle will
be urged by any Power which has an interest in
insisting upon it, and under any circumstances a
grave uncertainty is introduced into International
Law. But the Geneva decision, regarded as an international precedent, is open to much more serious
objection than this. As is well known, Great Britain
during the Confederate War was a neutral, and she
was condemned by the arbitrators to pay very heavy
damages as punishment for breaches of her duty as a
neutral. She was penally dealt with for a number
of acts and omissions, each in itself innocent. She
had a standard of due diligence applied to her neglects
which was new and extremely severe. And generally
she had a rule of neutral duty applied to her which,
if it has been really engrafted on the Law of Nations,
has changed that law materially for the worse. But
if there be one thing more than another which a true
court of international justice might be desired to
keep in view in its decisions, it is their future effect
on the rights of neutrals. Nothing tends to enlarge
the area of maritime wars so much as the neglect of
these rights. Nothing tends so much to make war

intolerably oppressive as any rule which helps, beyond what is absolutely necessary, to invade the principle that neutral states are merely states which have kept out of a calamity which has fallen on others, and which merely desire to follow their own business in their own way. From this point of view, the result of the Geneva arbitration is not happy. It turns back *pro tanto* the drift of legal opinion on neutral rights, which for many years had been setting in another direction. The Geneva arbitration, I repeat, conferred great benefit for the moment on Great Britain and the United States. But, looked at as a precedent likely to exercise serious influence on the whole Law of Nations, I fear it was dangerous, as well as reactionary and retrogressive.

I have dwelt on this aspect of the Geneva arbitration because it puts in what appears to me a striking light the disadvantages which attend these expedients for settling international disputes, through their being invariably brought into action merely *ad hoc*. A true court of quasi-justice, like a court of municipal justice, would be sure to consider the effect of a given decision on the whole branch of law which it administers. The defect, however, appears to me to be one for which it would not be altogether impossible to find a remedy. Many, indeed, of the innovations which have been proposed for the cure of palpable infirmities in the application of our Inter-

national Jurisprudence to facts seem to have but small
chance of adoption, at any rate in a society of nations
like that in which we live, through the magnitude of
the sacrifices which they would impose on particular
communities.   But no appreciable sacrifice would
have to be made by the single or corporate sovereigns
of the civilised world if they were to agree to constitute a single permanent court, or board, or assemblage of arbitrators, who should act as referees in any
questions which any community or communities should
choose to submit to them.   Such a court would not be
free from the infirmity which afflicts all such additions
to the international system.   It would have no force
at its back.   But I think it would be better constituted.   I think it would be more free from prejudice, and would soon be recognised as freer, than
the present occasional adjudicators.   And I think it
could be better trusted to adjust its awards to the
entire body of international principles, distinctions,
and rules.   Such a tribunal as I have described, a
court, board, or commission of arbitrators, having
a certain degree of permanence, might have all the
advantages which I have described for it—it might be
better constituted for its purpose than are the bodies
which are now trusted to conduct arbitrations, its
awards might be better considered with regard to
their effect on the entirety of the Law of Nations, and
it might be employed more freely as a body of

referees on critical questions which are now left to
themselves for want of any authority to which their
consideration might be committed. But still it would
not be a true court of justice. It would share the
characteristic, in modern eyes the weakness, of all
International Law, that it cannot command the assis-
tance of force. Its rules have no sanction. It cannot punish the breach of its rules or the violation
of an international duty. It is true that a defiance
of the Law of Nations sometimes draws down upon
the offender a very serious sanction, though it is indirect. Few sovereigns or states remain unmoved
by the disapprobation which an open breach of international obligation provokes—disapprobation now
rapidly diffused over the whole civilised world by the
telegraph and the press. Nothing could be more
satisfactory than the outburst of indignation which
occurred in 1870, when the Russian Government took
advantage of the difficulties in which Europe was
placed by the war between Germany and France, to
repudiate the restrictions under which Russia lay in
respect of naval action in the Black Sea through the
provisions of the Treaty of Paris, restrictions which,
it must be confessed, were not wholly reasonable.
The Russian Government had to abandon its position ;
and at a Conference of the representatives of Powers
who had been signataries of the Treaty of Paris, it
was declared that ‘ it is an essential principle of the

Law of Nations that no Power can liberate itself from the engagement of a treaty, nor modify the stipulations thereof, unless with the consent of the contracting Powers by means of an amicable engagement.' It is true that this assertion of the virtual perpetuity of treaties (to which an exception must be introduced, save by the effect of war) contains a principle which is not without a danger of its own. But the received principle is that which was laid down at the Conference. The truth is that an offender against the obligations of International Law is at present seriously weakened by the disapprobation he incurs. Nobody knew this better than Napoleon Bonaparte, who, next perhaps to Frederick the Great, was the most perfidious sovereign in modern history, when he persistently endeavoured through his official scribes to fasten on this country the name of 'perfidious Albion.'

But after all qualifications have been allowed, the denial to International Law of that auxiliary force which is commanded by all municipal law, and by every municipal tribunal, is a most lamentable disadvantage. The system owes to it every sort of infirmity. Its efficiency and its improvement are alike hindered. And in the last resort, when two or more disputant Powers have wrought themselves to such a heat of passion that they are determined to fight, the rest of the civilised world, though persuaded that the

contest is unnecessary and persuaded that its conta-
gion will spread, has, in the present state of international relations, no power of forbidding or punishing the armed attacks of one state on another.   The
great majority of those entitled to have an opinion
may condemn the threatened war, but there is no
officer of the Law of Nations to interfere with the
headlong combatants.   The amount of force which is
at the disposal of what is called the commonwealth of
nations collectively is immense and practically irresistible, but it is badly distributed and not well directed,
and it is too often impotent, not only for the promo-
tion of good, but for the prevention of acknowledged
evil.

About six months ago, when an Association which
has been formed for the codification of the Law of
Nations (which I may describe parenthetically as a
most excellent undertaking) was holding its meet-
ings, the subject attracted considerable, though only
momentary, attention.   An eminent French econo-
mist, M. de Molinari, published a proposal for what
he called a League of Neutral Powers.   The majority
of civilised states are always neutral, though the
neutrals are not always the same.   If the neutrals
combine they are irresistible, partly from their strength
and partly from their power to make one of two
belligerent Powers irresistible by joining its side.
M. de Molinari's suggestion was that it should be one

of the duties of neutrality to thwart the spirit of
belligerency, to make it a rule that the outbreak of
hostility between any two Powers should be a *casus
belli* as regards the rest, and to embody these arrangements in the stipulations of a treaty. It is impossible to deny that if such a combination of neutral
Powers could be effected under the suggested conditions it would be a most effectual safeguard against
war, and this is in itself an ample justification for
starting the proposal. But the objections to it are
plain, and were at once advanced. If carried into
effect, it might diminish the chances of war; but it
takes for granted that the mechanism of war will
remain unimpaired. If neutrals are to be equal to
their new duties, they must maintain great armies
and navies on the modern scale, or they may not
be able to cope with the contemplated emergency.
Thus, though the risk of war might be lessened,
the burden of war would at best remain the same;
there would be the same vast unproductive expenditure, the same ruinous displacement of industry.
One result of the scheme might, in fact, defeat another. It is not altogether true in civil affairs that
the strong man armed keeps his house in peace.
The fact that he wears full armour is sometimes
a source of quarrelsomeness, and a temptation to
attack his neighbours.

The scheme of M. de Molinari failed to command

the attention and interest which were essential to its
serious consideration, because it was too large and
ambitious. It was nevertheless founded, as it appears
to me, on a correct principle, that, if war is ever to be
arrested, it will be arrested by sacrifices on the part
of those states which are neither at war nor desire
to go to war. There is a very ancient example of
this method of arresting and preventing the spread of
war. Just before the dawn of Greek history, we
have a glimpse of the existence of several combina-
tions of Greek tribes (which as yet can scarcely be
called states) for the purpose of preventing war
among themselves and resisting attacks from outside. Of these ' amphiktiones,' alliances of neighbouring communities clustered round a temple as a sanc-
tuary, one only constituted on a respectable scale
survived to historical time, evidently in a state of
decay, and liable to become the tool of any aggressive
military Power, but still even then greatly venerated.
Now let us look around the world of our day, and try
to see whether we can find anywhere an example of
a successful amphiktiony, a combination of neighbouring Powers formed for the purpose of preventing
wars.

I think we have seen for ten years or thereabouts
a curiously similar alliance of the sort, framed for a
similar purpose. I refer to the alliance of the three
great sovereigns of Eastern Europe which is some-

times called the alliance of the three Emperors, which, however, they themselves do not admit to be in form more than a personal understanding. This alliance or understanding, if we may judge by the newspapers, is not particularly popular in Western Europe. Perhaps we do it the same injustice, and for the same reason, which as historical students we do to such great territorial aggregates as the Medo-Persian Empire under the Great King. Political freedom and the movement which we call progress do not flourish in these vast territorial sovereignties, perhaps through some necessity of human nature ; and thus we contrast them unfavourably with the Athenian Republic, the parent of art, science, and political liberty, or else with those modern societies to which we ourselves eminently belong. There is not much constitutionalism, as we understand the word, in Germany and Austro-Hungary, and there is none at all in Russia, and thus we are led to forget the services they render to mankind by the maintenance of peace and the prevention of bloodshed.

I suppose that, of the causes of war which we know to exist in our day, there were never so many com-bined as in Eastern Europe during the last ten years. The antecedents of the three combined Emperors were such as to threaten an outbreak of hostilities at any moment. Germany had waged a successful war against Austria, and also had inflicted bitter humilia-

Q

tion on France, till the other day the most powerful
military state in Europe. Russia in 1877–8 had been
at war with the Turkish Empire, which, though in
the greatest decrepitude, exercised a nominal sovereignty over nearly all of Eastern Europe which was
not included in the dominions of the allied sovereigns.
Among the small communities which were broken fragments of this Empire, the modern springs of war were
in perpetual activity. The spirit of ambition, the
spirit of religious antagonism, the spirit of race combination or of nationality (whatever it has to be
called), were all loose. Nevertheless, under these
menacing conditions, the ' amphiktiony ' of the three
Empires preserved the peace. We do not know what
were the exact terms of the understanding, nor do we
quite know when it began. There are signs of something like it having existed before the Treaty of
Berlin in 1878 ; and though it has to contend with
many difficulties (at this moment with one most
dangerous in Bulgaria), it is still said to exist. We
cannot doubt what the main heads of the understanding must be. The three Emperors must have agreed to
keep the peace among themselves, to resist the solici-
tations of external Powers, and to forget many of their
own recollections. They must have aimed at keeping
the quarrelsome little communities about them to the
limits assigned to them by the Berlin Treaty. They
have not absolutely succeeded in this ; but, considering

the difficulties, the success of the alliance has been conspicuous.

The precedent is one on which anyone who shares the hopes of the founder of this Professorship is forced to set the greatest store. It has been shown that a limited number of states, by isolating a limited group of questions, and agreeing to do their best (if necessary, by force) to prevent these questions from kindling the fire of belligerency, may preserve peace in a part of the world which seemed threatened by imminent war. It is not a very large experiment, but it has demanded sacrifices both of money and sentiment. It points to a method of abating war which in our day is novel, but which, after having had for about ten years the sanction of one precedent, is now in course of obtaining the sanction of another. For the alliance of the three Emperors is about to be succeeded by the combination of the Austro-Hungarian and German Governments with the Government of Italy. If, then, for periods of ten years together, one community or more, eager for war, can be prevented from engaging in it, one long step will have been taken towards the establishment of that permanent universal peace which has been hitherto a dream.

War is too huge and too ancient an evil for there to be much probability that it will submit to any one or any isolated panacea. I would even say that there is a strong presumption against any system of treatment

which promises to put a prompt and complete end
to it. But, like those terrible conflagrations to which
it has often been compared, it may perhaps be extinguished by local isolation.   In one instance at least,
when apparently on the point of bursting out in a
most inflammable structure, it has hitherto been kept
under.

INDEX.

PRINTED BY
SPOTTISWOODE AND CO., NEW-STREET SQUARE
LONDON

www.ingramcontent.com/pod-product-compliance
Lightning Source LLC
Chambersburg PA
CBHW030405270326
41926CB00009B/1281